BARE IN MIND
A Collection of Poetry

Scotty Bare

ISBN 979-8-89112-998-6 (Paperback)
ISBN 979-8-89112-999-3 (Digital)

Covenant Books
11661 Hwy 707
Murrells Inlet, SC 29576
www.covenantbooks.com

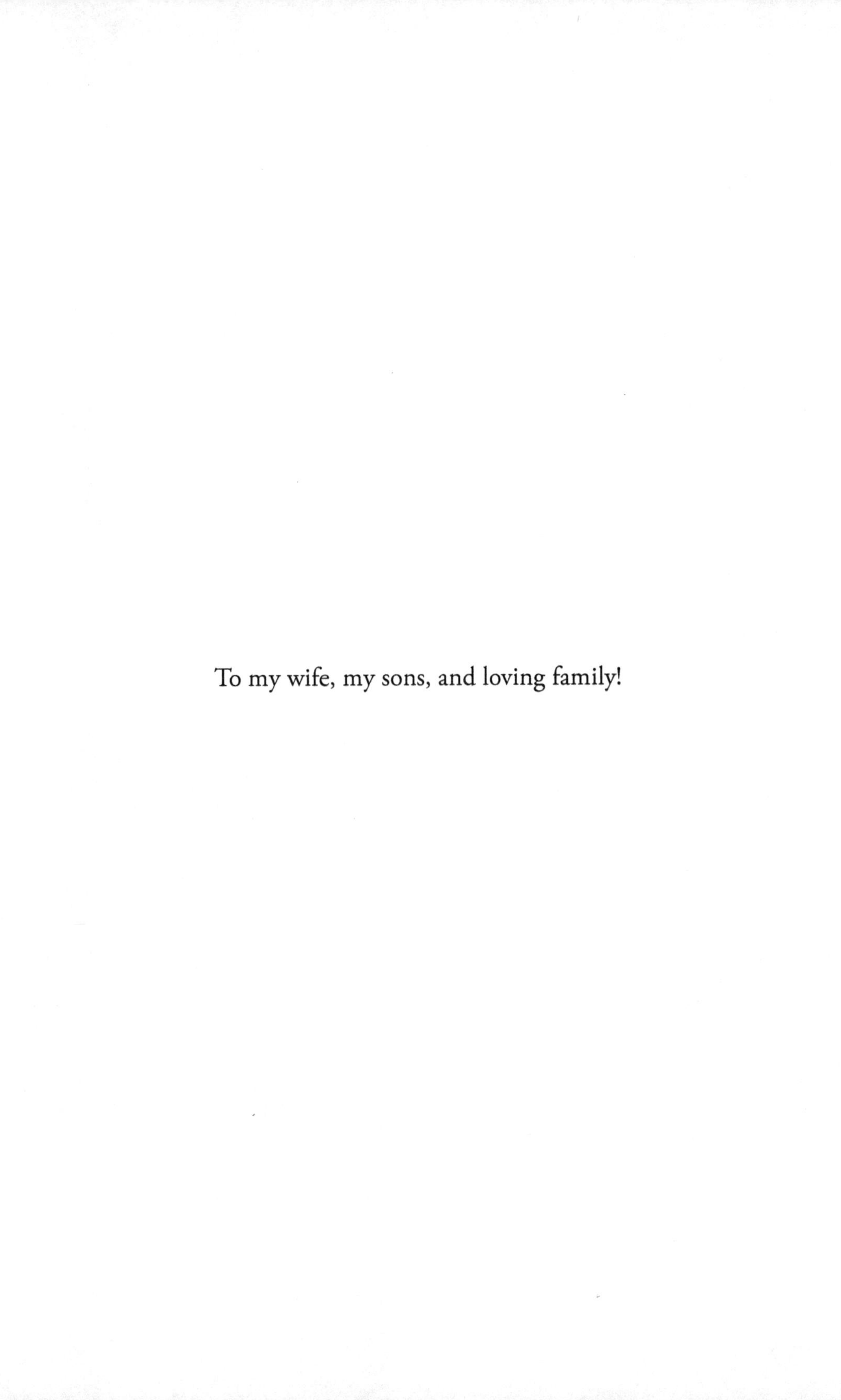

To my wife, my sons, and loving family!

Contents

A Crown for the Rose

The wilderness was where I called my quiet home. My fingers of thorns helped me live all alone. My only disturbance was sand from the wind, occasional man or beast life would send. My journey becoming this man's earthly crown began when a soldier's sword blade cut me down. Confusion then entered my mind as he said, "This crown will be perfect when placed on his head." Crowns were of silver, precious jewels, and of gold; crowns were of beauty I'd always been told. As he tangled my body, intertwined me around, I noticed a figure in blood on the ground. The solider moved close to lift up the head; I looked for a face yet saw crimson red. I pierced through his flesh as the soldiers mocked him, "Here's your crown, king, but your reign's looking dim." I've tasted before the shed blood of a man, the bitterness salt from his working hand. This blood tasted different, and that I am sure, this blood isn't bitter, this blood's taste is pure. They carried his body, entombed him in earth, as I lay aside because of my worth. My place as his crown, my thorns came to know, not for a king but a crown for the rose.

Be Still

What is the meaning, this scripture, "Be still"? All in existence contain not the skill. Laws of physics prohibit tranquil acts, defined by this science strongly stated as facts. All living things set in motion remain, to keep them as fixed cosmic law can't explain. Smallest of trees maneuver 'neath blowing wind, largest of trunks built with strength also bend. Slowest of sloths and slimy-shelled inching snail, fail in their life to contain sitting still. Waters lay calm yet gently flow its terrain, clouds seem as lifeless, move pouring earth rain. Even life's body lay on chilling death's bed, finds motion within until its pronounced dead. Thoughts in the mind also void of such sleep are scattered themselves in the shallow and deep. Again, at this question, moving mankind would ask, while devils attack, each mind hindering still's task. Keeping one still includes more than this flesh, requires our mind, body, then soul for success. Worldly distractions must set far aside, bitterness, anger, and most of all pride. The greatest ingredient to remain standing still, comes upon forfeiting heart's deceptive will. Accepting the plan of a much supreme force, instills deep within our life's spiritual course. Choosing to stand, instead of wilderness trod, reveals His divine presence. There we'll know He is God.

Brook of Kidron

Just beyond Jerusalem's thick stone facade, cutting dry valley ebbs the Brook of Kidron. Attaching small paths going both to and fro, stands traveled bridge over brook's water flow. Sitting due west on its high-mounded sod, this glorious temple erected to God. Detailed in stories paint red blood's dark scene; Passover's sacrifice fill waters once clean. Offered to God for Israel's past sin, carried by priests in gold cups to within. Passed down the line stood the first priest to last, saving spilled blood, every drop to be cast. Resting beneath altar's gold mercy seat, tunneled lamb's blood once atonement's complete. Still high suspended hung lamb's exposed flesh, soon would become sweet aroma expressed. Heading towards east pathway packed with hard clay, Gethsemane's garden walked Jesus to pray. Having a cup of his own placed in hand, crossed the blood waters seeking God's divine plan. "Father, if thou will please let this cup pass. Nevertheless I'll submit to what's cast." Thrice prayer was lifted while followers slept. Sweat became blood as obedience wept. Kiss of betrayal enters with his own cup, followed by soldiers as heart stayed corrupt. Crossing the last time walked God's faithful Son, passing blood waters, this Brook of Kidron. Knowing the fate that his blood too shall fall, enters Jerusalem lamb's blood for all. Again lamb suspended for all man to see, hangs salvation's fragrance that found even me! Flowing no more is the Passover's blood, into this brook walked over by love.

Cross That's Born Again

The beauty of my place of birth entails within one's eye, a forest green concealing roots left rotting soon to die. I am void of branching arms that grew most plentiful, now made into a wheeled vessel that working livestock pull. My outer coat's protective bark is gone just as each limb and sold to use upon the ground as decorative trim. The sole remaining part of me not having suffered loss was split in two then formed to make the executor's cross. My duty is much different than before when shading earth, which now is holding evil men that face death's stinging curse. I bear the holes of driven nails that once cut through man's flesh as crucifixion seemed each one a verdict of success. The vilest souls who spent a life-consuming ruthless act, claimed innocence as blood ran down my aging sun-dried cracks. Chose for me to hang today upon Golgotha's hill is one I've never seen so much desire for them to kill. His guilt I questioned from the start of death's cruel painful path, as all who came before him had resisted judgment's wrath. Willfully he carried me until his strength gave way, enduring with a joy that no other man's displayed. Knowing now I took my part in God's salvation plan. I was His cross, yet if not so, I'd be His cross that's born again.

Evil

Hearts deny God, which refuse He exists. I'll prove that He lives by love's opposite. First accept this, love comes by God's hand, not from your heart or created by man. Believers in science accept this fact true. If something exists, it's opposite too. Up has its down, down having up. Round holds a square and square holding round. Right going left, left then goes right. Nights turn into day and day turning night. Death's void of life with life void of death. Breath breathing in then out breathing breath. What devises a heart to heed evil's plan, just as with love it's not made by a man. Evil's dark plot has not been evolved, neither has love. Your mystery is solved! Science can't explain how one takes a life, neither can say what's causing world strife. So tell me, dear friend, if God don't exist, what's causing this wrong of love's opposite? How can a hand abuse a small child? Don't tell me that's science or time-lapsing compiled! If you believe man came from fish DNA, then why was there evil in fishman's first day? How can your fish go and enter a home then steal from more fish while evolving alone. Then your small fishman turned into an ape and somehow evolved into men who go rape. Foolish to think this man-made false belief proves God don't exist while providing relief. Let's not forget knowledge or wisdom to learn; I've yet seen a monkey gain diplomas it earned. I've also not heard drug cartels being run by monkeys who's making billions from drugs. What makes a mind think I'll go hijack a plane, crash into a building, or bomb a full train? How about a man that God deems a fool, who then takes a rifle and shoots up a school? What in your science class explains this cruel act, what fish did evolve to do such attack? Evolving defined means improving each stage, so why are man's actions going the wrong way? Believe what you will,

I just know you've been caught in evil's sharp snare and deception it's taught. Yes, God exists and forgiveness is true. Love's opposite of evil trapped you.

First Death

This cradle of death is familiar to most, just once in a life bearing mortal's chilled coat. Restrictions of age not part of death's law, a final life's breath is scheduled for all. Events for this man whose age is now old, mustn't be silent but unceasingly told. Diseased was my flesh, consuming this clay, and those that I loved were placed in dismay. A body of youth owned strength and endured, had withered away without healing's cure. Request was sent forth at my final hour, to Him that all knew possessed healing's power. Unknown to us all who were present that day, His sovereignty yet to be on display. My heart's beat drummed slow, it's time nearing stilled, lungs loosing air once plentifully filled. Sorrow and pain my death would create, loved ones discouraged His arrival was late. I dwelt in the bosom of Abraham's chest, my body entombed and soul set at rest. Four days in this journey I witnessed no pain, out in the distance then echoed my name. Instant restored my vessel's void soul, awakened my eyes to graves darkened cold. Garments of death unravel then fall; I stand in the presence of crowds still in awe. Smiling at me, a tear in His eye, the One others questioned in asking Him why? Passing long years, I feel once again, the stench of death's breath upon my old skin. Absence of fear, now hearing once more, the One who had brought me from my first death's door.

<h1 style="text-align:center">*Grace*</h1>

Traveling along this journey of grace, God's loving kindness resides every place. Morning awakens a gracious new day, darkness of night given grace as we lay. Forgiven by grace for each wrongful deed, faithfully granted by Him, which I need. Marvelous grace when sorrow appears. Healing broke hearts, while drying shed tears. Comforting grace during suffering's sharp pain. Holding together cut's open, wound's strain. Feeling alone, grace knocks on shut door. Reminding a soul grace is waiting once more. Questioning God, requesting again. Sufficient is grace defined for all men. Renewal of mind, grace places tall hedge. Evil can't enter that spiritual wedge. Feeling rejected, grace welcomes with hand. Walking along as an eternal friend. In times of fear, grace provides strength, forging God's armor for battle's long length. Grace will surround the doubting contained, laying within an uncertain brain. Grace is available for every need, for every prayer, begging, and plea. Needing salvation, grace always is there. Lay every burden, lay every care. Authoring grace, the Great Holy Throne. Even to some, rejecting grace shown. Grace freely given to all of mankind, not just his children is love's grace confined. Grace is unmerited by sinful filled men. Yet through His longsuffering, it's given again. Setting examples of how we should live, grace is an attribute we all must give!

Greatest Lie Told

The greatest of lies ever whispered or told wasn't by man, neither young nor when old. Said to the first, then all men that came, his lie never altered, remaining the same. Distortions of truth is this lie's pursuit, dispersed by each demon whom he did recruit. An atheist path this lie don't conceive, for even in fear these demons believe. The lie is more subtle and spoke with a grin. "No judgment awaits that's based off your sin." "Mansions in Heaven is where souls will dwell. Don't worry, dear children, you won't go to hell." A mind game of truths are partially spoke by evilness, tongues knowing Satan's cruel joke. "Give to the needy and even the church." Deception delivered with this false report. "Flames of hell's fire are only for those whose lives are much worse and cause many dark woes." Further into this lie masses fall, deafening their ear to Salvation's call. The father of lies continues to snake while slithering his way for you to forsake. Avoid the snake bite for its lie is but dead, as Truth has been spoken and bruised evil's head. Turn to the cross and to its work hold, reject in your heart the greatest lie told.

How Can I Pray

"How can I pray?" is asked by most men, moments of weakness reside deep within. God only knows your burdened, hurt heart, yet having others who could be a part. What's your request, no details I need. Just like to know on how to proceed. Sometimes a mind is blurred by much thought, making your prayer time sadly distraught. I too have faced this spiritual fight, in times of darkness while needing His light. Edify others the Bible commands, lift up the fallen by taking their hand. Pray without ceasing is tough in this life, each facing heartache when dealing with strife. Short is this poem, but hear my heart say, what do you need and how can I pray?

How

How, you may ask, can one display grace while turning their cheek after hate struck their face? How, you may ask, can a parent forgive at a killer's court trial when their child doesn't live? How, you may ask, can a spouse mend the pain brought on by unfaithfulness and its hardened strain? How, you may ask, can a friend grant hug's hold while lodged in their back is betrayal's blade cold? How, you may ask, can a victim still smile in suffering the worst from one who's hostile? How, you may ask, can an addict lay down a substance that nearly put them in the ground? How, you may ask, can a body have life that's filled with great joy as disease creates strife? How, you may ask, can the brave shield the shot of a bullet extended from evil's dark plot? How, you may ask, can a family take in a child whose real parents aren't able to tend? How, you may ask, can an officer tell a loved one they can't say their final farewell? How, you may ask, can pure strength fill the old to lift up their soulmate whose body can't hold? How, you may ask, can a stranger be kind while others keep walking and leave you behind? How, you may ask, can this world not wax worse as Satan is roaming as a lion with a curse? How, you may ask, can we all get along when many seek nothing else than to do wrong? How, you may ask, can a war end in peace when pridefulness causes the fight to not cease? How, you may ask, can these questions come true while selfish desires of the mind do pursue? How, you may ask? Well, the answer is sure; it all starts with love which is How's only cure!

I Adore

Beholding eyes cry often brings forth a why. What's causing tear's flow, while inquiring to know? Seeking your answer, please hear cry's reply, heartache and pain aren't the reason eyes cry. Something much better is stirring my soul. Thankful though you made an offered console. Sit while relaxing with listening so quiet, cry's not what's wrong yet what's made this life right. Blessed is the man walking right with each step, not that I'm righteous but Him I accept. I am not worthy receiving such gifts, viewing this list brings great joyful uplift. Firstly, upon this main reason to smile, looking above to my Lord facing trials. Without His death, I'd be lost in this life. Also not knowing His love conquering strife. Next, although pain has advanced since my youth, family and friends helped explaining God's truth. His hand of chastisement I too have felt, as a young man in a sinful world dwelt. Restoring grace poured from His gracious hand, revealing He had a more special plan. Married twelve years to my bride I so love, blessed every moment by God up above. Now little children are running amuck. Those unaware this is blessed, not pure luck. Sometimes not knowing where money will come, God shows back up and says, "Look what I've done." So undeserving of all he bestows, why He keeps blessing me, He only knows. Facing the enemy day after day, my only chance is God, you have your way. Loved ones gone on as my age grows in years, even in death I can show happy tears. Heaven awaits, and with His word I know, in this salvation, I too shall will go. Behold my eyes, and I'll tell you once more, I'm not discouraged, it's Him I adore.

Keeper of the Keys

I guarded the vilest, most wicked of men, confined to the strongest steel bars built within. Robbers and thieves bound to plunder no more, murderous hands tightly chained to my floor. No warmth of the sunlight or feeling wind's breeze, their hope for true freedom fades with each begging plea. Brought to my dark dungeon were two marked with stripes, I fastened their feet, both in stocks cold as ice. I entered my quarters embracing the quite, which lasted until the first stroke of midnight. An earthquake so great shook the foundation's bed, entered my thoughts were, "They surly all fled." Then knowing my fate, I drew out my sword's blade to thrust in my flesh for the error I made. Echoed from darkness, I heard a loud cry, "Lay down death's sharp weapon, we're all still inside." Amazed by their singing and God that they praised, desiring then asked, "What must I do to be saved?" They told of a man and I learned His great name, I bowed and believed then my house did the same. Washing the wounds of the stripes they endured, there's one thing I'm certain and will always be sure. Their cause not to run, nor escape or to flee, I never was truly the keeper of keys.

Last Day

Consumed life of waste filled with malefaction's dark shame now come to an end on this cross where I hang. Larcenist hands would persistently steal yet suffer today a pain most surreal. Quick were my steps while maintaining quiet feet, which now are constrained with a nail in defeat. Ignorance of mind in thinking this naive thought, "My crimes would be hidden, I'd never get caught." Death now my fate with two more on death's row, another poor thief, while there's one I don't know. His crime I'm not sure, yet it must be severe, his beaten, broke body made His image unclear. Although He was sentenced and judged in disgrace, the pain and the suffering He seems to embrace. Even more shocking as agony grew, voiced was "Forgive them, they know not what they do." Then realization this man was Divine, so wrongly convicted and placed here to die. Within a dark heart renewal finds a home that now understands I won't die all alone. Request I then made from a dehydrated tongue, "Remember me, Lord, as you enter your kingdom." Emanate peace now knowing the price, heard from his lips, "You'll see paradise." Breath quickly fading, my body's soon end, death stands before me, yet life had begun. Awaiting death's sting stand a crowd full of men, along with myself see my last day with sin.

Light

Heaven's canvas wields upon its never-ending page, illuminating forms throughout which light the dark pathways. Petite in size, the starry lights innumerable to count, draw constellations casting forth bright silhouettes throughout. Reigning blackened skies and shining down its borrowed light, an ever-changing moon eclipsing silence of the night. Sovereign burning rays that warm earth's seas and lands of clay, extends from sun while also rules and governs light of day. Distribution's purpose that's exclusive from the rest, of universe's objects each unfit to pass this test. Expelling darkness from the eye to clearly understand, the journey's path that lies ahead with laboring demand. Extruding roots and dangerous pits exposed by lustrous light, prevent the pains of errant steps, bring travelers much delight. Broken limbs from deadened trees that build their lowly arch, avoided by the guiding hand of light's protruding arm. Destinations soon obtained are possible to reach, the obstacles along pathways a traveler now can teach. The soul requires a lighted path yet not celestial glow, an undeserving luminous Word for all mankind to know. A destination promised way beyond these evil lands, a resting place of peace resides the House not made with hands.

Lost in a Suit

Please take your suit off, along with its tie. Reveal your true self and expose your life's lie. Inside the church, your appearance seems clean. Outside the doors your cold heart remains mean. Lifting up proudly yourself above men, who haven't a suit, yet have Christ deep within. They work free for widows, not telling a soul, while you shake her hand and continue to stroll. They give an earned hundred while being discreet. You place a greed's twenty, requesting receipts. They sit in each service, shed humble tear's cry. You're checking your watch with a boredom sleep's eye. Raising their hand giving praise during song. You roll an eye thinking, "This song is too long." They voice in preaching a soft spoken amen, while you get upset that the message is sin. He's hugging the preacher with thanks for Word's truth. You're patting his back unconcerned to show fruit. Listening to secrets from those you've deceived, saying you'll pray but in gossip proceed. While this poor man, having heard same requests, spends his night praying instead of some rest. No desire accepting the will of God's call, you begin peeking so you know it all. During this invite, you see the poor man, praying for you to submit to God's plan. Not even knowing his prayer is for you, your mind starts to wonder, "Just what did he do?" Heading back home, you hang up this false suit, then carry out your own evil's pursuit. While at another house, he hangs old clothes, giving great thanks that God's ear only knows. Now comes the time as death knocks at two homes, he sits in peace while you sit there alone. Wearing a suit you once gave the church drive. He's more than ever, not dead but alive. Now in a casket, you no longer dispute. Buried eternal and lost in a suit.

Love

Within her pure heart, a young maiden asks, "Just what is true love?" Declare this tough task. Desiring love's path also in mind, a gentleman's quest with hope he shall find. Also those old reflect on love's thought, remembering the time when they were first sought. Defined by the Greek come three forms of love. Agape, Eros, and lastly Philia. Structured the same yet difference avails, Agape's true love will always prevail. Its essence when found is fragrance so sweet, without this perfume our life's incomplete. Agape's embracement is void of man's skin, converging upon what lies deep within. Voicing a sound inaudibly heard, yet resonates tone expelled from His word. Its temperance stands kind, then envieth not, while suffereth long, provoking forgot. Paths sacrificial entirely in stride, desiring a soul where it can reside. A haven of rest built of durable stone, secure for each tenant who's never alone. Warmth for hearts hurting chilled by the hate's cold, wrapped in love's blanket, forever consoled. Hands of Agape so gently sincere, removes and then bottles each saddening shed tear. Its color of crimson flows purest of blood, supreme was the price of Agape's great love. Faith, hope, and charity found a lost soul. The greatest part gained resides charity's role.

People Don't Care

People don't care this world is distraught. People don't care that enemies fought. People don't care if evil is sought. People don't care, give nothing a thought.

People don't care this world is distressed. People don't care if people's a mess. People don't care to slow your progress. People don't care, it's time I regress.

People don't care this world is disturbed. People don't care that sin has occurred. People don't care that hate has emerged. People don't care, have this you not heard?

People don't care the worlds in dismay. People don't care that others betray. People don't care if families stray. People don't care, they will not obey.

People don't care this world has distrust. People don't care to share their own lust. People don't care their actions unjust. People don't care, nor want to discuss.

People don't care that sin does abound. People don't care that grace can be found. People don't care 'bout their ignorant sound. People don't care their spirit is bound.

People don't care, so why should I care? People don't care, so why should you care? People don't care, so how can they care? People don't care, yet we should all care!

People don't care I write about care. People don't care you cry about care. People don't care, so why care at all? People don't care, 'cause people don't care!

Sense of Faith

Faith provides substance, no evidence seen. Faith in what's hoped for as God intervenes. Faith requires total submission by man, using all senses beyond our own plan. Five designed senses, each one must perform, high upon mountain or tossed in life's storm. Outweighing each sense lives the presence of sight, eyes become first what the enemy fights. Deceived by Satan, "You must see this proof." Friend, look around, then you'll have no excuse. Eyes entail earthly sights named as temporal; what faithful eyes can't see is eternal! Faith comes by hearing the word of our Lord. Entering not mind but heart as a sharp sword. Listening just once does not grow a great faith, ears must allow His word entering each day. Taste and you'll see how the Lord is so good, sweeter than honey, poured from the best wood. His garments send forth aroma of myrrh. Once one breathes in, its aroma preferred. Reach to this garment, in faith feel His touch. Find in His presence agape's true love. Earth contains nothing where faith won't prevail. Yet without faith, the poor soul enters hell. "Well done, faithful servant," awaiting each face. Enter His glory by your sense of faith.

The Carpenter's Shoes

The days of my youth in sawdust were spent, freshly sawn wood and stain were my scent. Scared is my body from splinters of wood, protecting my owner as all good shoes should. My days of this work then suddenly changed; my days from here on would not be the same. It started quite odd; forty days we were gone; He continually spoke yet we were alone. His cry was "Dear Father," I'd heard this before, but not in this manner, I could not ignore. Amazed on our journey with each step we took, if my soles could write, it'd fill every book. Even for me, you'd never believe, that this pair of shoes even walked on the sea. Many the people that we came to meet, at one door I sat, a dame washed his feet. She wept and she cried while others did stare; she then dried them oddly using her hair. Others were healed, then some made to walk, blind made to see, the dumb could now talk. His favorite place we journeyed today, a garden where he would regularly pray. This prayer made me nervous, yet I did not judge, I noticed his sweat became drops of blood. An army took him and tossed me away, without my dear owner, here I shall stay. I've sat here for hours wondering what just took place, sounds of commotion I wish to erase. I see now the crowd and know where he's been; I heard that his body now looks like my skin. I thought to myself, he wasn't a shoe, what did he protect and what did he do? The conclusion I had was he went and saved those that he mentioned when he always prayed.

The Reader

If a verse in a day were read by a man, eighty-five years his reading would span. If he choose to read a chapter instead, just over three years, his reading will spread. If he were not to read the Bible at all, at the end of his days, what could he recall? If a verse in a day was understood by a man, eighty-five years God was holding his hand. If a chapter a day he held in his soul, just over three years he'd see God in control. If he did never read nor did he believe, when death comes to him, he'll see he's deceived. I suspect there are those who've rejected to read, whose ears still have heard and yet don't believe. I suspect also they reject in their heart, not knowing in judgment they'd hear this depart. A life for the reader will soon end in rest, peace, and enjoyment, a place with no death. For those that had sat the Word to their side, and choose that in life they would never abide, will soon find themselves in a place of unrest, a place of eternal darkness and death.

The River

My waters flow deception, I'm the River of deceit. Spring producing substance deemed by many tasting sweet. My shallow source is entered not knowing one will find, further down my widening stream drifts confusion of the mind. High my bank walls stand, restricting one's escape. A slippery slope and tangling weeds, addiction forming shape. A rippling current yield to rough, its course first motioned still, mold gentle men with self-control to men that aim to kill. Earth's strong members built a dam, force one to stay in place, against the wall, eyes peering at the passage of disgrace. Reflecting sprays of memories mist reveal a painful path, minds engraved and not erased by those who witnessed wrath. Soaked in despair and fighting through earth's jagged fallen wall, ahead awaits is clearly heard a crashing waterfall. A rocky landing fate's prepared to cripple one and all that drink this liquid as it laughs, my name is alcohol. Lakes are filled with guiltless acts performed without a thought as tributaries multiply the number I have caught. My forks instill a hope that this doomed journey's course may shift and falsely teach my riders that a better end exists. My mouth spews in deep oceans whose void of solid ground, deposit river waters to waves where one will drown. A way of rescue still exists, I call him enemy. If found the ship and anchor of the Captain of the Sea!

Thieves

Thieves desire not to rob empty home, profits not there so home's left alone. Gain is obtained by stealing what's yours, even great values, safely secured. Man holds greed's passion, stealing pure gold. Yet roams a thief attacking man's soul. Thieves prefer night, fulfilling desire, as Satan does in evil's attire. Those bought with blood have value matchless, giving this thief one to go suppress. Souls in God's hand can never be stolen. Yet taking joy, forever their goal. "If we can steal God's testimony, watch this witness send others to flee," said by evil, attacking the saved. Knowing its future, Hell's fiery grave. Armor is given, protecting our mind. Without God's shield, these darts many find. Stay in fight's battle, 'cause victory's won! Shouting the gospel of God's precious Son! Greater is He than he in this world. Be vigilant, one seeks to destroy. When attacks come by evil's dark face, tell that ol' thief, "I'm saved by God's grace!"

Tools of Crucifixion

If the hammer could talk, I'd imagine it'd say, "I wish I had hid when I woke up that day." If nails could shed tears, I'd imagine for three, enough shed to cause rust for eternity. If wood could have walked, I'd imagine two did, just as the hammer and woke up then hid. If cat-of-nine tails had eyes that could see, I'd imagine them closed 'til it was set free. If a whipping post had hands, I'd imagine its chains would have been removed to end all the pain. If tools had a voice, I'd imagine a roar, "Our work was quite joyful but not anymore." "Our duty is torture," I'd imagine they'd claim for those that are evil, those men cannot tame. "Something is different," I'd imagine they'd write, why this man refuses to put up a fight. Anguish, I'd imagine they'd be at His death, as this innocent man took his last breath. If tools had a conscience, I'd imagine the thought, "Why into this plan we're sadly now brought." If tools had a soul, I'd imagine they'd know, they just accompanied God's ultimate goal.

What Do You See in This Storm

Today I set sail on a journey just as the day just before and the one before that. The waters of life do my vessel rest on, my heading a path which I always have gone. I stand at the stern as the wind sets my speed, while sun shining rays on my face then proceed. It seems that my voyage this day will be still, and all of my plans I will surly fulfill. The sea life is calm while the birds fly in peace, waves formed just only by my ships release. Storm clouds then brew in a blink of an eye, the sea life dives deep and the bird's wings don't fly. The sun disappears and vile darkness arrives, the wind's breath once calming is one that now thrives. My vessel no longer sails with such rest but tosses and turns in a life of distress. My plans have been detoured in this great state of grief, my only desire from this storm is relief. The sky's bolt of light is now my only resource to manage this vessel along its rough course. Now thoughts of this day make me question my path, could I avoid this storm's evil wrath? My coordinates are lost as my eyes peer around, looking for just one small evidence of ground. Frantically racing is my heart's strong beat, I run to the hull in a state of retreat. Sounds of the storm are all my ears hear, a journey once started with joy now is fear. Not knowing my fate, I then peak out the hull door, the fear once within isn't there anymore. At the ship's stern stands my captain's bright form, who then asks me, "What do you see in this storm?"

What's My Prayer

What's my intention and what is my thought, what's in my mind and what's in my heart? Am I so selfish of only my need missing in others while soaking in greed? Even worse are prayer's wants, I crave forgetting of those near poverty's grave. I sit in a place that for many would seem as a palace and throne that's fit for a king. I feast at a table lacking hunger's demand as beggar's desire one bite from my hand. A coat in the cold and warm heat fill my home, while homeless are frozen and die all alone. Heat of the sun is cooled with paid air as others are suffering, which isn't that fair. Have blessings of God made me as a man one who forgot there's a much bigger plan? I've taken for granted day after day, not giving you thanks and neglecting to say. Vain are the words of selfish request denying the pains of other's distress. If answered by God was my prayer and plea, would change be the worlds or only just me?

What's Up

What's up is now down and down is now up. What's turned inside out is now right, not corrupt. Right was once right and left was the same, directions gone wrong are what we've became. One, some will say, now represents two; a mind so confused, common sense found in few. A boy once a boy who shook with a strong hand now thinks he's a girl doubting God's divine plan. A girl who once skipped as her hair danced each step, despises her beauty that she won't accept. A man was once thought as someone who was tough, now puts on a dress and a blouse and some fluff. A woman once known as a virtuous soul, now lives in a life that deception has stolen. Love shown now seems to be taken as hate, accepting false truths that they do create. What's known being right is now deemed as wrong and wrong is now right where God don't belong. Sky is now ground and ground is the sky, this world's upside down, and it makes us ask why? Square is now round and round is a square, what makes individuals seem unaware? The rainbow was made as a promising sign, yet now is rejected as solely divine. Destroying the plan of a true family is what we've become in society. We live in a world that's grown so corrupt; again, in my mind, makes myself ask what's up?

Where Are They

Positioned in silence stand a sequence of souls, their anticipation with eagerness grows. Beyond the vast crowd merry eyes do behold, heaven's bright throne that John had foretold. Reflecting flames of fire burn from lamps before the throne, seven spirits gleam, sounding thunder strikes a tone. Beneath lies crystal waters, a glass sea that mirrors peace, Holy, Holy, Holy rings aloud from mouths of beasts. Beautifully is sitting, resembling jasper stone, He the rightful owner of this great and mighty throne. Consumed with heaven's beauty are faces known to me, whose hearts have longed for ages of this place we humbly see. The search begins for those I loved and mentioned when I prayed, yet visions fail, an absence tells the question, where are they? My place has now advanced in line, before the throne, my judgement time. Deeds of life become my case, my Christian acts of love and grace. Before my eyes though, names displayed, the voice of truth asks, "Where are they?" "The ones instructed from my tongue, for you to tell I am the One." Again He asks me, "Where are they?" My shameful cry, "I disobeyed." "Lord, they stand in a separate line, rewards of work you'll soon decline." A Great White Throne of judgment waits, souls to enter Hell's dark gates. Pain of torments fill Hell's ear, but listen close and you may hear, "While on earth," their souls do say, "I asked in quiet where are they?" "The burdened who possess the truth but failed to share with lame excuse." This dream of horror, I now awake, eyes filled with tears and hands that shake. "Lord, guide my heart to be not dismayed," to sinners who's asking Lord, "Where are they?"

Why, Jesus

Questioning, "Why, Jesus?" I too asked the same. Prior to understanding love, before my soul was saved.

Questioning, "Why, Jesus?" continue rejecting truth. Deceived by evildoers, who could care less for you.

Questioning, "Why, Jesus?" "Where's the evidence?" Without real proper research, believes false intelligence.

Questioning, "Why, Jesus?" "Religions swarm this earth." Void of realizing, Satan gave those birth.

Questioning, "Why, Jesus?" "Judgement time's a myth." God's courtroom is not as one man can plead the fifth.

Questioning, "Why, Jesus?" "Such sacrifice is lame." Confused about humanity, man's sin is not a game.

Questioning, "Why, Jesus?" "God wouldn't reject me." You're right, He won't! You're the one, rejecting Calvary.

Questioning, "Why, Jesus?" "I live a decent life." Maybe then we'll worship you, since you're the one "divine."

Questioning, "Why, Jesus?" "No place exists named Hell." Once more deceived, explain in depth how evil is propelled?

Questioning, "Why, Jesus?" "Hypocrites claim Christ." Some exist, I agree. They'll face their own harsh price.

Questioning, "Why, Jesus?" "Keep your fairytale." Please keep in mind, the gospel's truth always will prevail.

Questioning, "Why, Jesus?" "Men pinned down your book." All I suggest is that you go and take another look.

Questioning, "Why, Jesus?" "science proves Big Bang." Really? I must ask, why don't things continue change?

Questioning, "Why, Jesus?" "Evolution is correct." Explain then how humans came to know a love's respect?

Questioning, "Why, Jesus?" "Christians just go judge." You defined this judgement, what I have told is love.

Questioning, "Why, Jesus?" "I committed too much wrong." Who told you that, they don't sit upon a righteous throne!

Questioning, "Why, Jesus?" "Can my lost soul be saved?" Just like many others, it's only through true faith.

Questioning, "Why, Jesus?" Don't let last words be spoken. Once you hear the word depart, you'll know it's not a joke.

Questioning, "Why, Jesus?" Cast away to flame. This question being the last one, having asked in shame.

Questioning, "Why, Jesus?" It won't be His hand's fault. Giving truth, accepting lies your soul has sadly bought.

Questioning, "Why, Jesus?" I'll give my last reply. I cannot speak for you but know why Jesus had to die.

Questioning, "Why, Jesus?" Don't ask very long. We're all unaware when we'll go out singing our last song.

Why Do You Tell Me

Why do you tell me this heart displays hate, when I'd give my last dollar knowing you had not ate? Why do you tell me my words echo strife, when softly I've spoken for my entire life? Why do you tell me I act without love, when no man I've ever in anger did shove? Why do you tell me my mind cannot speak, when each person living is made quite unique? Why do you tell me my knowledge is small as I too have hanging degrees on my wall? Why do you tell me my soul is a judge, when I'm not the one here that's holding a grudge? Why do you tell me I think I don't sin, when daily in prayer I ask God to forgive? Why do you tell me I think I'm perfect, when I know there's much that I need to correct? Why do you tell me I'm wrong to believe an innocent child is a life when conceived? Why do you tell me that I should stay quiet while those for your cause burn down cities at night? Why do you tell me I can't think that a boy will always be one, no matter his choice? Why do you tell me this same thought for a girl who I feel is only confused by this world? Why do you tell me opinions cause pain, we all possess them and they're rarely the same? Why do you tell me I can't think that a man should marry a woman, which is part of God's plan? Why do you tell me believe in your science when a family is made just by man and his wife? Why do you tell me I'm old fashioned in thought, it's not from the old but God's teaching He taught? Why do you tell me your hypocrisy's dead when you accept all but what Jesus has said? Why do you tell me I'm wrong when I train my children to know this world's corrupting their brain? Why do you tell me you'll live how you please, then question your life when it's not one of ease? Why do you tell me I can't say what I deem as true, if you only knew it's because I sure love you? Why do you tell me you can't be my friend, which only proves more that I'm right in the end? Why do you tell me I can't have my own voice while you are the one who's created great noise? Why do you tell me I'm ignorant to say, when I've studied God's word yet you push it away? Why do you tell me my love is unreal, when it's your deception I try to reveal? Why do you tell me to hold my own breath, we'll both know the Truth once this life has found death!

Wounds of the War

Moonlight's dim presence paints the darkness of night. Sounds of earth's life have become mostly quiet. Echoing hands of the clock's lingering tick, cause eyelids to close as the weight of a brick. A dwelling of sleep a tired body then flees, an active mind paused now is resting in peace. The comforting ease abruptly then dies, the body awakes as something arrives. The whispering voice speaks so small and so still, requesting my path would include His great will. A second voice speaks yet not as the first, this voice seeming fierce as though spoke with a curse. My mind's instant change develops into a field, as battle ensues and its weapons revealed. The arsenal choose was not blades of sharp steal, arrows nor bows that so accurately kill. Waring of words as one voices "submit," the other fights back claiming "do not commit." A household of rest are away in a dream, as I lie in anguish and silently scream. "Reveal it, dear Lord," I proclaim with demand, passion's desire to know my future's plan. Exhaustion gains strength with each slow passing hour, the moonlight's dim glow slowly loses its power. Another night's war has now come to an end, sunlight's reminder a new day began. Concern floods my soul, do not cease in your prayer, all Christian soldiers face the same fight's despair. My helmet repaired and armor restored conceal with its strength painful wounds of the war.

Another Day Around the Sun

Eyes awake before clock's scream, once again removed from dream. Sunrays bounce across the room, shine which shows this life resumes. Muscle's stretch begin blood's flow, time's alarm now sounds its crow. Body rises from bed's warmth, shower waters thus come forth. Time clock punched starts active work, break time brings relieving smirk. Stress builds pain between each joint, mindset not to disappoint. Clock strikes noon for needed meal; conversations help each heal. Hours done as whistle blows; workload somehow seemed to grow. Daydream slowly starts to bring, thoughts removed by phone's loud ring. Coffee once more flowing hot, soon resides cool empty pot. Conference call to end hard day, workers part and go their way. Home contains a restful seat, moments gone as back on feet. Chores lay wait to be performed, children once again are warned. Table sets a peaceful place, void of life's swift moving pace. Questions how each day has been, some had losses, some a win. Evening playtime now arrives, hopeful those involved survives. Setting sun let's each one know tiring bodies start to slow. Cleanup needed once again; prayers completed by amen. Rest resumed with all now done, another day around the sun! Closing eyes, now one on one, another day around the Son.

My Mind

My mind's built as a tilt-a-whirl, with thoughts that quickly spin. Around and round and round and round and round then once again. There is thoughts about my family, also of all my friends. Ones of church and thoughts this world is coming to its end. If my age makes eighty-five, will my face look the part? Will I still be as awesome or an ol', sour, hateful fart? Am I healthy, what's this pain? Are just my kids crazy? Why am I shy, refuse to cry? Why's people so lazy? If outside and have to pee, will anybody see? I'm hopeful that this squirrel don't turn around and soon bite me. What's for lunch, where'd my money go, I thought I just got paid. Gas is high, I need to mow, I'll soon need to go shave. Should I go back to college? I'm probably way too old. does Duke play ball this weekend? I wish they'd pave this road. Another mass shooting came across my app's news feed; they're faulting guns, but I know Jesus is what the shooter needs. Could I run for office? Probably not, I'm too honest. I'm ready for five o'clock, still probably can't go rest. Am I called to preach or just to study and go teach? Did I fail to mention lunch? What time should I go eat? Two minutes have passed by since this silly poem began. I think I'll start it over and try to write again. Man, I love pizza and good ol' country ham, pintos, and great cornbread. Do I want more? Oh, yes, ma'am! Our government's a laughing joke. Should I go find new work? Have I mentioned lunchtime? Man, this dude's a real rude jerk. What's God's purpose for me? Do I raise my kids all right? Green Bay better make the Super Bowl. My garage needs a new light. Should I replace my bumper or leave the dent alone? Have I just spoke the last words to a friend I've known so long? Should I move my family or remain within this place? This shirt is way too small for me. What's this bump upon my face? What song to sing or station on my radio to play? Should I take lessons on guitar? Where is lunch today? Have I succeeded in my life? What age can I retire? I love this dog and is my life a life that does inspire? Do others read these writings? I'd love to learn Hebrew. I think that Spanish would cool and learn some Latin too. I really like this movie. This popcorn's a bit stale. I wonder what it'd be like if I spent a night in jail. This insurance is confusing. Am I a good husband? What's the best investment? Some things are hard to understand. I'd like to have a cookie, chocolate chip always the best. I need a long vacation; my mind is needing rest. I lay awake and wheels still turn, and what's that noise outside? There's friends I miss from younger days, what have they done in life? Time goes fast, memories made, I hope I have been kind. I'm thankful for events that give me something for my mind.

Cornbread in Heaven

Eyes vaguely peer towards far distance of past, laid upon burning eye skillet, iron cast. Missing from scene is sweet-smelling cornbread. Sitting alone waits young boy to be fed. "Granny, where are you?" such sadness is heard! Waits for reply, yet quite silence gives word. Rising from table, he walks, empty room, knowing she's there with aroma's perfume. Calling again as voice cracks in dismay. "Granny, it's time to eat, please be okay! Where is your laughter, compassionate grin? If you're here speaking, speak loud deep within." Once more, he turns with his heart's seeking quest. Beholds the corn meal, again makes request. "My hand's unable in baking like you. If you're not coming, then what will I do?" Sinking reality deep in his soul, just as his empty ceramic bean bowl. Closing both eyes pulling memories to mind, hearing a voice he remembers as kind. Having distractions, he covers both ears, knowing this voice is one he wants to hear. "Hello, sweet jackass," she says with quirk's smile, giving this nickname when he was a child. "Seventeen years since I died in God's plan, open your eyes, boy, you're now a grown man." Unwilling to listen with fear she will leave. Eyes remain closed, every memory he cleaves. "I miss our joking," he says with shed tear. "I know God's taken you, please come back here. Everyone's tried to make cornbread like you, yours is the best!" Knowing this statement true. Further he speaks pouring out memories past. "Can we just sit as you crochet and laugh? Tell great life stories," continuing on. "How about singing our favorite bean song?" Feeling such guilt for the time he stayed home, "If only I knew that next day you'd be gone." Knowing his painful days weren't quite the same, says, "Listen real close and I'll gladly explain. My hands don't tremble, these fingers don't hurt. I don't hunch over, and no longer work. I have no aching, my body's renewed. I'm doing great,

I'm just waiting for you!" Voice much familiar yet image diverse, no longer pictured with aging's old curse. Knowing time's short, asks her this last question, "Can I eat please, your cornbread in Heaven?"

Daddy

Before your first cry, I could hear your heart's beat and, listening so close, also heard kicking feet. Desire amplified by that precious small sound; I could not await until you were around. At last you came forth ringing sweet toning cries, while holding you close as glad tears filled my eyes. Nerves growing high as my thoughts formed within, settled back down by your calm, smirking grin. Some sounds you made were not pleasant to smell but made this dad happy you were eating so well!! Then came the cackle of darling laughter, a sound bringing us to a new life's chapter. Producing the song as a sweet melody, a laugh in my mind I pray always will be. Next came the fussing while you learned to say no, a sound that I knew you were starting to grow. A shout and a whine you had put in your plan, while I try to mold you into a great man! The toys went from bright lights and musical notes to bouncing of balls and us cracking dad jokes. The sound of bike wheels turning on our concrete then cries when you crashed not too pleasant or sweet. Yet sounding out joy when you rode all alone that melted my heart as you beat an unknown. Pattering feet are now thundering steps as you run and jump over every object. Your voice of a baby has changed to the tone of a bright little boy who too quickly has grown. Reading out loud and you counting so high make me understand that time surely does fly. One sound that's unchanged is from me and holds true, the words in my heart saying I sure love you! Sounds of your life make me feel quite happy, but the greatest I hear is when you call me daddy.

Empty Chair

Fixed in room's corner beyond draped window, sets empty chair beside lamp's softened glow. Dressed in upholstery, knitted cloth fades, wood marked with scaring throughout long decades. Void of an occupant these countless years, waiting yet there remain no volunteers. Fragrance emitted from each single stitch, weaved in chair's garment aroma so thick. Memories gained by each passing this seat, stop and close eyes so this memory repeats. Face now appears and familiar voice heard, image so clear that before was slight blurred. Eyes quickly open for life to resume; steps are continued and leave empty room. Left in quiet background remains empty chair, with its aroma still floating in air. Unlike its fabric, no feeling cloth has, yet if that is true, this soft fabric would cry. Fixed in a Kingdom where moth don't corrupt, rust not destroying a mansion's construct. Within this mansion beside Golden Street, lives an aroma now Heavenly sweet. Fixed in room's corner without world despair, gladly you rest in your new empty chair.

Momma's Boy

Call me a momma's boy all you need to. She taught me to fight, and she could whoop you! On a serious note, how about a thought's ride? Down memory lane, as we close our eyes. Traveling back to a most wonderful year, nineteen eighty-one with spring growing near. This world wasn't ready for what just took place, entered this writer with a B-E-A-utiful face! All right, I was kidding about the "serious note." Let's enter this journey, please pardon my gloat. A mother's pure love is so often compared as the closest embrace to God's love and His care. I witnessed this truth every day of my life, even when actions caused my momma strife. Let's start at the first then we'll travel to now, so you'll understand and too realize how. My mind can't remember the days after birth. Although I think hard, memory doesn't come forth. Seeing in snapshots the picture of love, previously mentioned that came from above. A young mother holding a son (which was me), love gleaming from her glad eyes plainly seen. My first memory was when I had turned three, I fell off a swing cause a spider scared me. Back from the ER with stitches sewn tight, she cleaned up the blood, laid me down for a good night. Then came the divorce once my age was near eight. I'm sure some can sympathize and closely relate. Four, now residing almost a full year in a two-room apartment where love was still clear. Providing our needs and cool things she still done. Y'all had the money, but we had the fun! Cooking so good like prepared for a king, hearing her beautiful voice gladly sing. Working her fingers right down to the bone, making sure Christmas was wonderfully known. Life became busy yet she still made sure, when church service started, we walked through the door. Finally we gained a new home of our own! Bicycles, ball hoop, and yard to go roam. Washing and cleaning and then once again, then cleaning and washing, good Lord, say amen! Hid in my hand was my school free lunch card but knew in my heart as a child she worked hard. Driving to daycare and 4-H each day, seems like she always somehow found a way. Taking us shopping each fall before school, not wearing the best, but we still looked dang cool! Vacations were great, except one not at all! The time we went swimming and her top came off. Ladies and gentlemen, let's please take a break, a moment of silence for this anguish…okay! Where was I at? Oh yeah, that's she's great. Even played jokes like buttered nose on birthdays. Giving us chores we neglected each week, teaching to love, although sometimes life's bleak. I wish I knew then just how quick time would fly. I missed many moments to sit by her side. I'll be really honest, when I moved away, I struggled with leaving and had some heartache. Yet even in college, she made sure that I knew, how mommas still cherished their children who grew. Having now children myself, understand the love she has shown helped me be a real man. If titled a momma's boy my entire life, I'll take it and grin knowing you're probably right. The virtuous woman who raised this ol' boy, done more than most men I've met and with great joy.

Failed

I've failed as a father, I've failed as a man, I've failed as a son, failed as a husband. I've failed as a brother, I've failed as a friend, I've failed since the first and will fail 'til the end. I've failed as a worker, I've failed to obey, I've failed as a leader, I've failed not to pray. I've failed as a teacher, I've failed not to learn, I've failed to lift up and failed showing concern. I've failed to sound laughter, I've failed not to smile, I've failed not to sing and failed to go the last mile. I've failed in the winter, I've failed in the fall, I've failed not to answer, and I've failed not to call. I've failed in the summer, I've failed in the spring, I've failed not to hug, and I've failed not to cling. I've failed to show happiness, failed not to cry, failed to be helpful, and failed not to lie. I've failed as an athlete, I've failed not to win, I've failed in contentment and will fail soon again. I've failed in my service, I've failed to proclaim, I've failed in my witness, I've failed not to blame. I've failed reaching goals, I've failed to stand tall, I've failed to accomplish, and failed most of all. I've failed in my faith, and I've failed to be light; I've failed in my trust, and I've failed not to fight. I've failed in my study, I've failed not to grow, I've failed not to listen and failed to let go. I've failed as a Christian, I've failed to show love, I've failed to forgive and failed all this above. I've failed not to mention, failed not to inform, I've failed 'cause I'm human, I've failed in the storm. I've failed to be perfect, I've failed to maintain, I've failed not to hurt, failed not to feel pain. I've failed to show mercy, I've failed to give grace, I've failed to go forward and failed to keep pace. I'll fail to the grave, fail 'til my last breath, I'll fail here no more when this body finds death. There's only one area I will not fail; it's not from my doing 'cause I deserve hell. I'll fail not to enter a heavenly home; my soul cannot fail because Christ I belong.

Fearfully and Wonderfully Made

You're ugly, you're fat, you're poor and worthless, you're skinny, you're dumb, just look how you dress. You're dirty, you stink, you're such a huge freak, useless, stupid, you're wimpy and weak. You're a slut, you're a whore, you're better off dead, you're creepy, crazy, you're probably inbred. You're goodie-two-shoes, a dork, you're a dweeb, you're nerdy and weird, please go away, leave. You're unpopular, gross, you're unattractive, you're geeky, you're plump, so why do you live? You're brainless, a chump, an idiot too, you talk funny, walk funny, people hate you. You're uncool, you're a dope, a dim-witted goon, you're lame and retarded, hope you will die soon. All right, that's *enough*! Reject these false lies, ears hearing words that produce hurtful cries. Listen real closely to what's really true, you're made in God's image, He surely loves you. You're not a mistake, you're made by design with hands that are Holy and solely divine. You're beautiful, special, you're made most unique, turn from cruel words of such evil critique. You're confident, loved, you're precious in sight, you're cherished, you're you, you're made with delight. Adored, you're cherished, you're life's of value, don't listen to words meant to harass you. Hate not yourself, don't be deceived, accepting His love brings forth something you'll see. Fearfully made means to reverence above, wonderfully made by God's hands to be loved!!

Can You Push Me

"Dad, can you push me," said running with joy, as I smile knowing you're now a big boy. "Yes, son, I'll push you, but try with your feet. Kick them out forward, then back and repeat." Chain starts its squeaking the higher you go, mind starts to think, "How can this be so?" Last week you barely could climb in this swing, how can such difference with time sadly bring? As my hand waits on your next swing's return, I start to ponder on all you will learn. As you get older, the less you will ask for my assistance in facing each task. One thing to know is I'm standing nearby and reaching out when you're struggling to try. Lessons are taught even from a small swing, lessons I hope this life always will bring. You just keep kicking no matter what comes, even if difficult still have great fun. Life's larger swing you will face as you grow, but Dad's still here when you think you can't go. On this small playground, I hear your laughter, knowing that one day we'll close this chapter. Is it today that I'll push my last nudge, as you've got older with such strong courage? Is this the last time my dad eyes will see or hear this child say, "Dad, can you push me?"

Hate

I hate the hate before my own eyes, atrocious dark deeds that I so despise. I hate the hate expelled from the lips; a tongue's delight achieved with cruel tricks. I hate the hate enforced by one's hand, a painful dark mark across this whole land. I hate the hate that's roaming the earth, its footprints reflect the hate's evident hurt. I hate the hate listening ears sadly hear, producing revenge only caused by its fear. I hate the hate's stench and foul-smelling breath, breathing avoidable sorrowful death. I hate the hate, its bite of deceit, ripping the heart with evil's sharp teeth. I hate the hate, its crippling long claw, scratching away while ignoring God's law. I hate the hate and what it can't see, all having our flaws, especially me. I hate the hate and what it can't say; forgiveness and mercy they do not obey. I hate the hate's hands and how they place away, affectionate sculptures to ever display. I hate the hate and where it won't dwell, a neighboring home, there just to rebel. I hate the hate ignoring to hear, love God and love others commanded so clear. I hate that hate allows in its mouth, rejection of grace so blinded by doubt. I love to hate so many decide, refusing to set any difference aside. I love to hate are people who live, a bitter lifestyle that's so negative. I love to hate would cease I do guess, if understood all have this sinfulness flesh. A hate to hate becomes a life goal, when love enters willfully into a man's soul.

I Have Kids

Why's there popcorn on my lap? How are fruit loops in each crack? What's that screaming in my ear? I hear fighting, do you hear? Why's the laundry piled so high? Where's my snacks I went to buy? Why's my eye began to gaze? What day is this, my mind's a haze? Why's my floor look like Walmart? I smell something, did you fart? What are these markings on the wall? Where'd the dog get one more ball? I need sleep, why am I tired? Where's my wife, did I get fired? How'd the kitchen light get broke? What's on fire, I smell some smoke? Where's my sheets go every night? Who has broken another light? Why's there toothpaste on the glass? Who keeps digging up my grass? Who keeps stealing my flashlight? Where's my wife, is she all right? Who is watching these cartoons? Who keeps busting these balloons? Why are there clothes thrown on the floor? Who put stickers on the door? Who threw gum on the sidewalk? Where's my wife, we need to talk? Oh my gosh, who broke this light? Weren't the dining room walls white? Why's there broke crayons in my truck? Who keeps quacking like a duck? Where's my money, it's all spent? Who put crackers in the vent? How'd the quite turn into noise? Who keeps buying all these toys? Who left open the fridge door? Where's the ketchup, we need more? Why's there grape juice in my bed? Who poked holes in the new bread? Nighttime's here, a new day done. All I did was run, run, run. I found my wife reading to little boys that know they're cute. Now I know who made this mess. Vicious turds that make life blessed. All my questions now lay hid. I'm so thankful I have kids.

I Have Not a Dream

I have not a dream for I lay awake, oh, the sorrow with burdened heartache! I have not a dream hurt eyes plainly see, hate is alive in such high degree. I have not a dream while loathing persists, wondering if love will ever exist. I have not a dream as ears hear once more, those which are grown act worse than those born. I have not a dream these colors of skin, look beyond flesh of what rests within. I have not a dream my flesh was made white, why would that color be reason to fight? I have not a dream your skin was made dark, which is no reason for hateful remarks. I have not a dream all sides are to blame, not wanting to see God made us the same. I have not a dream race isn't sole trap; many divisions are found on earth's map. I have not a dream as politics sting, take the gloves off and step out the ring. I have not a dream my children will know, how to treat others wherever they go. I have not a dream, I know how this ends; peace will not happen till Jesus descends. I have not a dream yet still I desire, people not hate and others admire. I have not a dream a difference we see, Lord let this not be a value in me. I have not a dream all wake up with sin, there's just one difference some aren't born again. I have not a dream stop causing such strife, you have one chance to live a love's life.

Where's My Baby

Turning around I don't find your wood crib. Where is the basket once holding each bib? How 'bout wool booties worn tight on small feet, also the diapers stacked up nice and neat? Who hid the paci and baby bottles, also the blanket where you were swaddled? Highchair is missing and bouncer is gone, where are the Boggans so wonderfully sewn? Rattles and burp cloths went missing as well, also it seems there's a more pleasant smell. Where is the baby swing and the wipes box; lost is the stroller which I liked a lot. I hear no cooing with laughing small sounds, where is the play mat once laid on the ground? A little boy is now in your old room, calling me daddy dressed in a costume. Looking once more yet unable to see, turning again I ask, "Where's my baby?"

I Know

What do I know and what should I know, there's things I don't know yet things I do know. What do I know, well, first, I'm a man who's made my mistakes with both tongue and with hand. Not singling out just these God given two, but my feet sometimes know not what they will do. Oh, wait, there's some more that's had some miscues, my mind and both ears have messed up plans too. I know that you know what I know is true if you know this life from this point of view. One thing I do know is I do not know all I should know so there's room to grow. The next thing I know is I want to know things that I do not know so my mind will then know. You know what I mean if that know you seek to soon know of the things that are most unique. You know what is odd there's things I do know that I know is vain for my mind to know. You know this void know if you know it's so vain and know that I know of thoughts useless domain. What I should know I know is my fault not looking to know when I could have been taught. I know there are things you also should know but just as like me you sought not to know. I know I'm not perfect and know I can't be but know I'm forgiven and know I am free. If this you don't know I want you to know that you also know the forgiveness I know. How can I know you may ask so you'll know my answer is simple I know that I know. I know that God loves me and know of the cross where I came to know that I know I was lost. I want you to know this if you do not know so you know this love that I also know. I know you're not perfect and know you can't be I know there's for-giveness for you just like me. Here's how you can know what I know in my heart know God sure does love you and know that's the start. Then know what I know that I know I've done wrong then know what I know before your life is gone. I know you can know cause He wants us to know then you'll know as I know and God's love you'll then show. I know what you know that's not important to know you'll know what I know and know how to grow. Don't know what I know and let its light fade know how to shine light and know others need saved. I know I have mentioned I know in excess, but let me explain my thoughts nonetheless. What do I know is the question first asked I want you to know and to know of love's act? I know there is nothing I can do on my own and know you can't either so you're not alone. I know that I love you and know not what you do but God sure does love you and you can know too. If you know what I know, I know that you know to tell it to others again so they'll know.

I Was Me

For my loved ones who all know, just what this man is like. A poem not filled with Scotty hobbies but what rests inside. I embrace the fact I'm loved, know others find disgust. I believe true words when spoke but found some heart distrust. I enjoyed fall's laughing hurt, upset with goals I failed. I can't stand a mouth that's rude, love words spoke with details. I have strived presenting love yet know great lack exists. My heart has suffered painful past, which healing hands transmit. I desire for monstrous wealth, yet not one cent for me. This same desire with burdened heart, to start a charity. I even have an awesome name, if fortune does succeed. My wish in helping others so it's "Bare Another's Need." Great music brings much comforting, my soul needs each played note. Writing is a therapy, with each word mind has wrote. I sure despise a racist heart; each race includes these fools. I also hate, with love, someone who treats another cruel. I have such high discomforts thought, while standing with a crowd. Not knowing what the issue is but feel my minds a cloud. My patience fuse is short in length, I pray its length will grow. Instead of aggravation's grief, I want my anger slow. I'm slow to shed a crying tear, though tear comes quick sometimes. Mostly when my thoughts go back with memories brought to mind. My Christian life's important most, then next my family. I hope to serve until my death, each one unsparingly. I give God credit for each thought, He's placed in this skull cap. Although I joke, while telling mom, it's due to youthful rap. One, two, three and to the four, Scotty Sawyer Bare and his brain is at the door. Ready to make an entrance so back on up. Or there ain't no party like a Scotty Bare party, cause a Scotty Bare party don't stop. Okay, I'll now stop. I aspire my acts through life, each long, short echoing day. To lay aside self-righteous mind, with judging eye's proud gaze. I, myself, with life's struggles, have bathed in small wash tubs. Warming water atop wood stoves, so how can I then judge? I grimace at the site of clothes, with wrinkles shown throughout. I tell my kids but do the same, please stop your whining pout. Probably the worst distaste that gives my nerve a chill. The sound of crunchy teeth chewing, is this your soul's last meal? I find a loathing in my gut, when words I must repeat. Take the time to listen please, it's not a laborious feat. Let's forget this negative, move on to sunny rays. It warms my heart when morning breaks, to hear bird's singing praise. I could stand on mountainous rock, forever view steep slopes. Or stand upon the sandy shores, observing this grand scope. I'd rather take an airplane ride, with parachute to see. The wonders of creation, yet Rosanna won't let me. I'm just kidding, she probably would!! I think what's best for everyone is sharing how they feel. Even if you tell yourself, this thought sure is ideal. I'm not meaning your self-pity; you're blessed beyond deserved. Take the time and think of life, and where your heart can serve. The greatest sound I hear in life is I'm so glad you're home. Knowing there stand many men, who walk through doors alone. It breaks my heart to read the news, see chaos roam around. What breaks it more while hurting worse, not calming each sad sound? I love you all and have my faults, but thanks for grace you've shown. When I'm old, I hope also my grace you too have known. Write these words on my tombstone, so dead can plainly read. "My resting soul resides at home! Here lies Scotty, I was me."

If I Find Old Age

My life here on earth is near half complete, if forty more years remains my heart's beat. Journey's time passed since it first began, once held as babe now known as a man. Appearance of flesh has visual change; smooth skin disappears with lines it obtains. Darkness of hair once danced in the wind, snowy white mix with dark now its blend. Seasons of change with each passing year, eyes seeing joy, and occasional tear. Lessons are learned at each setting sun, when taught to another, born is wisdom. Life I suppose cherished the most, sweet memories made my mind gladly host. Reflections of thoughts even frequently seem, as though I am watching them on a large screen. There's drama, laughter, adventure, and love, each part does include what life is made of. A heavenly home my soul longs to see, yet wondering what tomorrow may be. A story of pain, famine, poor health or happiness, joy, exuberant wealth? As God takes His finger to turn my life's page, just what will it read if I find old age.

I'm a Teenager Now

I'm a teenager now! Thirteen and know I don't need your help, will you let my hand go?

I'll be fourteen, only ten more long days, I can't do a thing! Gosh, I hate your old ways!

I am fifteen now, I'm almost grown up. I'm hanging with friends; please don't you interrupt.

I am sixteen, will finally go where I please. I deserve freedom and living with ease.

I'm seventeen! Why should I go find work? My youth's about over, don't be such a jerk!

I am eighteen, dude, it's sooo about time! I'm ready for college where I can live life.

I am nineteen but I kinda miss home. It hurts me to think you're there all alone.

I'm now the big twenty. Should I call to say? This bill is passed due, is it something you'd pay?

I just turned twenty-five, need your support. You'll meet your first grandchild, I'm glad to report!

There's no way I'm thirty, watch out for shed tears. Wish I could go back to my teenager years.

How am I forty? Oh, Lord, I now see! This difficult child is exactly like me!

How do I say in love to obey! Will they be like me, having learned the hard way?

Ten years have gone by, my children are grown. Now I am the one sitting here all alone.

I see your health fading; you're not doing well.

I know your time's short, but there's so much to tell.

Thank you for being a parent so great. Forgive me! I hope that these words aren't too late.

I just got the call, God, I'm asking you please! Let me hold to the hand I once bit that fed me!

Kids I Do Not Know

Faces come upon my screen, faces I have never seen. Each one holds a charming smile, each one rocking their own style. Every eye extruding joy, living life each child enjoys. Then I see what's written above each picture and written with love. Cancer has been diagnosed, prayer is now desired the most. As my heart is torn in two, thoughts arise, "What would I do?" I, myself, have precious sons; what if cancer reaches them young? Tears then flow and sympathize, as each parent testifies. Words of sorrow filled with strength, each one gave that makes me think. If I could, I'd ease the pain. If I could, I would explain. If I could, you'd hurt no more. If I could, I'd close that door. If I could, I'd cure your health. If I could, I'd stop each cell. If I could, I'd pay each bill. If I could, I would until. All I know is I will pray and continue every day. If I'm needed, please then ask, and I'll try each wanted task. God is faithful, this is true! God reveal what you can do! I may never meet these kids, yet my prayers will not be hid. Things I sure don't understand yet know there's a greater plan. Cancer sucks, I hate it so. Thoughts hurt more with children though. You don't know, yet rest assured, I am praying for this cure. Love is what we all must show to these kids I do not know.

Letter from Me

If given a chance and opportunity arose to write to myself this chance would be chose. Foolish the name I'd be given I guess by critics who claim this act was useless. "The past is the past, you should leave it alone," yet my heart would change decisions gone wrong. Beginning to write, I'd speak of love shown to those in my life where death's bed is home. No day would I mention of their final heart's beat ensuring love gave was not incomplete. Message relayed of "It won't be too long, so cherish the hugs before they are gone." Next on the list is the subject of time, naive in the thought, "Those moments were mine." Wasting my days on such selfish desire while watching once more opportunities expire. Asking, "What did I miss?" my mind never shall know, yet maybe this letter will help me to grow. Third on the page I would write of the pain I suffered and hid yet still they remain. Each one I would tell so I could prepare myself for the hurt brought on by despair. Following pain, my hand would then pen the wrongs that I made to not make again. Result from the choices and actions I took are now understood of how foolish I looked. Erroneous ways a young mind amiss, decisions while weak I could not resist. To prove that I lived and did not destroy my life I'd expound on all of the joy. The laughter I voiced and memories I made are those in my mind I pray never will fade. I'd tell my young self to focus and try, to not sit and ponder while questioning why. Also I'd write to not be afraid, be shy or so quiet but strong and more brave. I'd sign my long letter then add this PS, "Your life has been great and how God sure did bless." Then knowing what's wrote had developed this man, I'd have to then change opportunity's plan. Placed in a fire of the hottest degree, now lay the burnt ashes of my letter from me.

Nature's Sweet Chord

Roosters crow loudly proclaiming with rhyme, repeating his warning beginning showtime. Soothing tones echo as morning breaks dawn, bird's orchestrating new melodies song. Singing glad praise with harmonious sound, giving sweet beat hopping bunnies dance 'round. Sounding loud horns cattle slowly go graze, joining the meadow deer closely survey. Winged instrumentalist playing quick notes, frogs deeply bellow bass exiting throats. Working behind the scenes form marching ants, floats in the background geese resonate chants. Wishing to join the band singing off key, hyper dogs spinning around the tall tree. Approving with attitude cleaning its paws, felines meow softly retracting sharp claws. Livestock start mingling, producing great herds, swaying along as each measure is heard. Needing a rest from sun's heat of the day, chorus now paused from a horse's long neigh. For intermission and needing some sun, snakes slither out having missed all the fun. Foggy creations form filling the stage, buzzing bee's stinger cuts through the green haze. Mankind in awe of this daytime's first act, heads to concessions enjoying a snack. Sitting in silence comes pondering thought, lessons those singing unknowingly taught. Animals cared for by sovereignty's hand, better for man is our God's divine plan. Encore brought forth by wind clapping each leaf, evening's performance brings needed relief. Chirping small birds start announcing to all, sunset's approaching horizon's ground wall. Insects with locus set night's calming mood, rising moonlight has once more been renewed. Closing this show hooting owls perched on high, letting exhaustion's voice hum its soft sigh. Nighttime's creation creak whispering feet, delivering strums pitch so mankind can get sleep. Prior to eyes closing prayers sent to the Lord, thankful for hearing His nature's sweet chord.

Picture of Home

Escape's solitude from a world of distress is hung from the sky and quite picturesque. Vibrant bright colors paint scenes of the land, brushed with the stroke of His great divine hand. Seasons of change grant a different hue as onlookers see this most wondrous view. Stillness of water create mirror's smooth glass which reflect the sky, the trees and earth's grass. Vessel's propelled across this lake's veneer produce a soft roar until it disappears. Campfire is mixed with the smell of this place and burn memories that minds can't erase. Echoing tones that nature gloriously plays are symphonic sounds of this orchestra's praise. The notes enjoyed most from my listening ear are my children's laughs from abundance of cheer. Free from all worry their innocence plays with energy seeming could last many days. A picture of home hangs out in my backyard, a picture that I will never discard. Nailed to the sky for all eyes to look on is my favorite scene, my picture of home.

Scream

I scream, you scream, we all scream, but why scream? I scream, still scream, yet despise ice cream. You say you scream just for more ice cream. Yet scream is seen for more than ice cream. You screamed, threw a scene, when received wrong ice cream. Then screamed, obscene, to the whole shop's team. Your scream, loud thing, screaming that's extreme scream. We scream, all scream, blowing off some hot steam. This steam, some deem, merits a return scream. Some screams, hurt esteem, killing hope for real dreams. No gleam, then seen, vanished from the eye's beam. How mean these screams thrown around as evil schemes. Some screams carry themes, inviting more to share screams. Many screams filling streets, unity now unseen. Screams supreme, and won't agree, spilling blood which flowed envy. Hateful screams tear the seams of garments worn once scream clean. Only God can intervene, calming those with anger's scream. If allowed by enemies, we must place Him in between. Is a scream formed by genes or taught by only the obscene? Either way, screams must ease, or our screams will still convene. I stand redeemed, man should scream, instead this scream seems unseen. I scream, you scream, we all scream but stop screams. My dream is no screams, your screams and my screams. I scream, you scream, scream though for ice cream!

Seconds

Seconds build minutes and minutes set hours, hours produce time, then time forms moments we share. Days construct weeks and weeks conceive years, years design memories shaping memories held dear. Mornings give seconds rushed by love's goodbye kiss, those rushing few seconds through daytime lips miss. Evening gives seconds for conversations; discussion sets forth the next day's expectations. Nighttime gives way for useful seconds of rest, including love's passion two bodies express. Journey gives seconds for touching of hands while interlaced fingers join once more our ring bands. Happiness gives my eye seconds to see, two soft smiling lips where my mind can then flee. Laughter gives seconds to drown out the noise, ears escape turmoil this cruel world employs. Eyes give clear seconds to wonderfully gaze into a pure heart brighter than the sun's rays. Embrace gives sweet seconds for arms to wrap hold, encouragement lasts until both obtain old. Feet gives the seconds to join on a path, helping to guide so both fail not to crash. Tears give the seconds to shed away pain and comfort in seconds when life's unexplained. Marriage gives seconds placed by divine word, to have and to hold sees a family emerge. Life gives me seconds enjoying a home, as children are raised, immense love you have shown. Age gives us seconds reflecting time past, the beautiful seconds too quickly gone fast. Unreal in this thought yet if asked by the Lord, "Child, is there a part you'd repeat from this world?" As one having ate a meal without objections, I'd say "Lord, how about you please give me seconds."

Skin's Voice

Answer me this, which troubles my mind, just what about me produces divide. I haven't a voice to cause such dispute, my suggestion for all is you remain mute. The color of eye is seen by the same but varies in shade, yet I am to blame. Extended from me grows painted hair's strand, but I entice those who won't understand. The hue of them both cause you no debate, once more I am asking why my hue you hate? Our makers design intended a use, although I believe it wasn't abuse. My benefit warmth and protective tough coat is often ignored, overshadowed and smote. Distinctive imprints upon my terrain are meant for unique but suffer disdain. Sun's scorching rays I'd rather endure, compared to hate's pain, of this, I am sure. The gash of a blade don't equal the blood that's spilled to the ground with loathing's great flood. Suffering a bruise from object's strong blow fails when compared to hate's ugly show. I'm asking again why bow to such sin, I'm just as your neighbor, go make him your friend. When asked of this kindness and where it has been, request true forgiveness for fearing their skin.

Soldiers at Peace

"And the rocket's red glare," most eyes haven't seen, living with freedoms in thankless routine.

"The bombs bursting in air," rare scenes known by few, except those on battlefields seeing this true.

"Gave proof through the night," endless time clock of war, neighbors here fight shedding blood on our shore.

"That our flag was still there," grave's casket now drapes, family shed tears overwhelming heartbreaks.

"Oh, say does that Star-Spangled Banner yet wave," burned lay in ashes deemed an unpatriotic display.

"O're the land of the free," wanders radical hate, cursing in freedom these grounds so irate.

"And the home of the brave," resting soldiers at peace, receiving my thankful salute that won't cease.

Some

Somewhere, somehow, some try, some now. Sometimes some ways, some fail some days. Someone lonesome somewhat succumbs. Some win fearsome, some lose wisdom. Some place, some face, blossoms some grace. Some are handsome, some seem loathsome. Some set some goals, some dig some holes. Some deal, some steal, some fake, some real. Some pray, some stay, some die, some say. Some are awesome, some so tiresome. Some look gruesome, some more wearisome. Some live wholesome, some cause burdensome. Some like quarrelsome, some not troublesome. Some are noisome, some quite meddlesome. Some go, some show, some fun, some slow. Some dance somersaults, some sit, some fault. Some greed, some lead, some plant, some seed. Some are irksome, some adventuresome. Some read, some write, some love, some fight. Some work, some don't, some help, some won't. Some smile, some cry, some mind, some buy. Some push back some, some lay cuddle some. Some care, some stare, some are somewhere. Some saved, some lost, some give, some cost. Somehow, someone show some compassion. I'm done, some see this poem as dumb. Some see, some things, some joy some brings.

Three Siblings Play

Snapshots of time flood old, stored picture books. Offering free access to past's different looks. God provides choices mankind can decide. Except a home's family His hand will supply. Gifting some brothers, some sisters, some none. This brother's snapshots contain more than one. Two lovely sisters my picture books hold. Open this album and see what we told. Placed on the first page is pictured first born, curly blonde hair and a pink outfit worn. Turn to the second and see there's now two, a brother was born and his outfit is blue. Flip to the third, now lay pictures of three. Two precious sisters with brother, that's me! Amanda, I'm Scotty, and Julie our names. Memories held dear hang in wall picture frames. My biggest sister gave laughs without end, making sore stomachs I sure recommend! My little sister, which she'll always be called, gave joy filled moments that weren't little at all. Three amigos, picturesque in each shot, grew up together and went through a lot. Memory-filled pages show three siblings play, memories in mind is where they'll always stay. Summertime filled with Ashe Park and a pool. Wearing fluorescent clothes, yeah, we're that cool! Cooler's packed tight by our mother each day. Barrel juice, Doritos, and PB&J. Sometimes she placed a Capri sun for snack, along with a fudge round when money weren't slack. Playing red-rover and tie-dyed T-shirts, canoeing and camping with no harming hurt. I'll take that one back, they were not the ones harmed. I, for some reason, stayed in the ER. Spending the evenings in fields playing ball, inviting our neighbors including them all. Riding our bicycles up on the hill, ate Chilly-Willy's till our bellies were filled. MTV, VH1, played music to see, laughing at Mom not fond of "I'm too sexy." Sometimes my mind wishes I had one day, my sisters and I were young so we could go play. Taking our turns in the car's lone front seat, fussing and saying, "It isn't your week." Time spent at Nanny's in sleeping bags gone, but not the fun memories childhood had sown. Sledding in winters down snowy steep hills gave precious moments and times with such thrill. Watching great movies while down on the floor, if given a chance I'd reopen that door. Singing with Mom and at Dad's sounded great. Fighting each other when we were irate. Blessed in my life having both you weird dorks, how we got older gets me outta sorts. I could continue, yet eyes won't let me. There're filled up with tears, I no longer can see. Even now grown there's one phrase I've still said. You mess with my sisters, you'll find yourself dead. Pages remain for our pictures to grow, when we get old for our children to show. What they will hold, this cool brother's not sure, but I can sure promise that we'll help endure. However, I know pictured on the last page. Is Heaven's picture where these three siblings play?

Turtle Upon a Fence Post

A grandfather's son tells the story of old, his grandfather's son passed down long years ago. These lessons of life taught by wiser old men, are now seem forgotten as youth breaks the trend. It's told many ways but my favorite remains, as told by the farmer who gladly explains. While plowing his fields each blade carving hard ground, he gives the horse, "Whoa," hearing plow give odd sound. He sees on turned ground with shell bottom exposed, a scared little turtle with body enclosed. With moonlight approaching and needing work done and having compassion like grandfather's son. He places the shell on a fence post to rest, creating a scene humorous, nonetheless. Drivers pass by, view its curious shelf. Thinking aloud, "It did not get there itself." This same situation, I also found shared, with lovely encouragement, love's touch and care. Some came from family, my friends and pastors. Then from great teachers who taught I mattered. I've been richly blessed and deserved no kindness. Without life's assistance I'd sure be a mess. I, in life too, found myself turned upside down, thankful for those who picked me up off the ground. I'd never be placed at this point in my life, if not for the grace I had facing tough strife. I thank my dear Savior who helped me the most, I'm just a small turtle upon a fence post.

What Do You See

Hello, dear friend, hope you have a great day. Before I take off, there's just one thing to say. What do you see while you're looking at me, does failure reside or successful stories? What do you behold when you glance in my eye, is joy evident or pain deep inside? Is there a smile to begin this great day, or sorrow from knowing the world's in dismay? Do you see one whom the Lord has so blessed, or misery caused by the unending stress? Is there a heart you detect love extrudes or one only selfish and seemingly rude? Do you see compassion, warm and so kind, or witness cruel leaving the hurting behind? How about the change from the years on this earth, does wisdom exist with a knowledge of worth? The aging you see and the wrinkling dry skin, have they spent a life always being a friend? When you take a glimpse of the gray mix of hair, was it placed there only by worldly despair? When you see the scars and the pains gained from years, do you realize many came from shed tears? Do you notice happiness, peace and great cheer or do fussiness, bitterness only appear? What about grace, is it recognized shown to others in life or to them an unknown? How about Christ is He something one sees and puts in their heart a desire to believe? Or do they perceive it's a false acting love and claim it is something they don't want a part of? Is there a thankfulness heart on display or one that in nothing will appreciate? I know you can't answer these questions at all, for you're just a mirror that hangs on my wall.

Library Lost

A book void of parchment containing no ink, nor sets upon bookshelves where thinking minds seek. No smooth binding leather supporting each page yet held strong together by wisdom's old age. It's often forgotten while left home alone, that once housed their children now scattered and gone. The ignorance of youthfulness sees wrinkled skin yet needing to read the words hidden within. The pages of this book are written with tears, that's penned down with pain's blood shed many tough years. Its cover is blank yet clear title is shown, so wisely spelled out with loud wrinkling skin's tone. The truth of its words vocalized and not read yet stands near no reader to hear what book said. Wrote from its beginning throughout till the last, are words of experience gained from the past. This knowledge and wisdom then laid down to rest, is gone from all readers who missed their request. Unfortunate minds seeking now know the cost, of such priceless wisdom, this library lost.

Bait

Earth's first known fishermen seeking their prey, fashioned devices still useful today. Whether a wooden rod, net, or thrown spear, catches were baited by each pioneer. Some caught quite quickly with perfect made bait, others with patience while learning to wait. Bait often weighted to reach waters deep, light weighted bait for those easily reached. This is the focus of choosing great bait, casting before every fish swam away. There's application applied to man's soul, catching the lost ones gave Christians our goal. Now brings the question which causes debate, what should all Christians be using as bait? I read one answer by God up above, written at Calvary spelled out in love. Dragging by net makes the fish run away, never returning as predators slay. Throwing a spear only cuts the fish skin, putting resentment to God deep within. Placing sharp hooks while it's ripping fish jaws, doesn't show God's love defeating His cause. What should we then place inside tackle box, one thing for certain not self-righteous rocks! Nor artificial bait works for man's heart, you must yourself obtain real bait to start. Catching a soul caught out in the world's sea, requires not wounding but God's loving plea. As we are called to this fishermen's role, let us bait others with what caught our soul. Living a life while we share Heaven's truth, baiting each fish so they'll have no excuse. Fashion together God's grace through your faith, so many fishes can be caught today. Each fish that's caught never shall be thrown out, nor suffer death from an evil caused drought. Earth's first known fishermen swam in sin's flood, caught not by their bait but redeeming blood.

Bare Hands

What could I give, concerning my child, from my estate which I have complied? When I find death and enter Heaven, will I leave joy or leave depression? Wealth not obtained to ease their burden, look for yourself behind closed curtain. Silver and gold reside in a land, far from my own I work with my hand. I have a mansion built not on this earth. Things that I own, rich never see worth. What I will leave, dwells not in large banks. I'll leave them this, be able to think! Have some integrity dealing with man. Show great respect, both them and women. Grant love's compassion to those without. Have sweet humbleness, leaving no doubt. What I possess, I testify sure. Life's full of troubles you will endure. Not by yourself, if you so request. There is a helper giving you rest. I'll leave a laugh, continue it please. Give to your children, set them at ease. Generations desire to pass on, something of value when life is gone. Work hard my children, knowing this fact, slothful lives lived, remain off the track. Have hands with scaring, even calloused. Setting life's goals, is always a must. Lastly, I'll leave my name and this plan. Pass to your children, loving bare hands.

Beat the Clock

Time to wake, time to shave, time to bathe, time to pray. Time to brush, time to floss, time to dress, no time for loss. Time to go, "Hey, let's go," time to leave, "Get dressed, let's go." Time to eat, time to pee, "Wash your hands, gosh, honestly!" Time to drive, time to poop, turn around, "Please hurry too!" Time to wipe, and again, "Go back up and wash your hands." Time to leave, "Come on, dude! I forgot to give dogs food." Time to leave, "Buckle up," time to sing, "Don't spill your cup!" Time for school, time for work, "Stop your honking, crazy jerk." Time for coffee, "Make that two," time to wait for it to brew. Time to read, time to write, "Who sends emails through the night?" Time to draw, time to add, "Engineering ain't too bad." Time for break, time is up, time for lunch, "I've had enough!" Time to breathe, time is small, time for one more conference call. Time has come, once again, time for coffee, "Say Amen!" Time to finish, time is gone, time to play, "Yay, Daddy's home!" Time for dinner, "Wash your hands," time to wash the pots and pans. Time for soccer, time to pack, time is over, "Let's head back." Time for washing kids and clothes, "Where's my wallet?" No one knows! Time for homework, time to chat, time you tell me, "Who broke that?" Time for cleanup, time for bed, "Dog is put up and been fed." Time for brushing, time to say, "Now is not the time to play!" Time for scripture, time to pray, "Now it's time to hit the hay!" Time for quiet, time to smile, time to hug this precious child. Time for lights out, time now free, time for thinking, God and me. Time for sleeping, time for two, time for arms to go hold you. Time is ticking, and a lot, wake once more to beat the clock!

Color of Dust

I have yet seen written carved on tombstone, mention of looks or skin's coloring tone. Eyes just attend only seeing a name, above two dates of death and when birth came. The visual color is blandest stone gray, certainly as the dead flesh with decay. Those without flesh buried long from date shown, doubtless have only the color of bone. Buried together and seemingly true, bodies no longer share different views. No longer categorized how each appear, known once as opposites now as death peers. Bringing together the races of earth, death killing prejudice forming at birth. None walking through the graves ponder within, "Was this flesh color a light or dark skin?" Also not questioned by those passing by, "What did they look like," yet "How did they die?" Finally seen with a sympathy's cry, not as a color seen through a blind eye. Death is appointed to each beating heart, reflect true love prior to riding death's cart. What all should see is not blatant disgust, but every skin is the color of dust!

Edge of the Storm

Two friends stand gazing upon the seashore, discussing life just like always before. Each special memory told with a shed tear, also great blessings and things they both fear. They have grown older and time's passing fast, no longer youthful with twenty years past. Still waters suddenly crash with great force, sun rays now vanished with clouds changing course. Quickly clouds gather and take a dark form, these friends now gaze at the edge of the storm. Now gusting winds twirl at high rates speed, one gets entangled and pulled out to sea. Feeling quite helpless the other alone, runs down the shoreline with heartache that's grown. "I cannot reach you," cried loudly with fear. "Please keep your head up so my voice you'll hear." Then he that's standing sees drifting at sea, two wooden pieces nailed forming a tee. Anxiously waiting as his friend is tossed, yells out encouragement, "Cling to the cross. Hold to it tightly and let it lift you, only that rugged cross can bring you through." As the storm's raging now over both men, lightning and thunder increase with strong wind. "Keep fighting," comes from the one on dry land. "I know by faith, you'll soon stand on soft sand." Waters now easing and winds calming down, waves thrust the cross with the clinger to ground. Then comes the other with warming embrace, both kiss the battered cross for saving grace. Laying exhausted they see a great sight, with the clouds breaking shines through the sun's light. Each understanding the sun never left, but only hidden by stormy distress. Two friends stand gazing upon the seashore, rejoice on seeing the edge of the storm.

Eye of the Beholder

Image perceived as grotesque by vain fools, speaking maliciousness utterly cruel. Thoughts gave obtained by society's mind, looking through magazines poorly defined. Those with deformity each page omits, told their gross image must not be submit. Some with obesity called a "fat face," told undeservedly, "You have no place." Others looked on being short or too tall, those even skinny told, "never at all!" Worldly obsession to fit a fake mold, making a mind feel it's less in control. Listen up closely and give a good ear, there stays in this world great truth you must hear. Marketing doesn't reveal what is real, publishers' only present false idea. I'm here explaining what each face should know, words brought to relevance long years ago! Wrote on the pages of this Holy Book, don't take my word but let's all have a look. "Let us make man in our image" composed "after our likeness," the Godhead imposed. Don't let illiterate people define what God created in perfect design. Glance in the mirror, repeat after me, "Who is this person my eyes plainly see?" Here is the one and the only answer, seen in the eye of the great beholder. You are so beautifully made by design, one who has loved you so seek and you'll find. Beauty is not what this world has acclaimed but is what God made forever proclaimed.

Eyes of Angels

Titled as Gabriel, archangel of God! Scrolls for your knowledge have I supplied not. Scriptures inspired willed by God's divine hand, observed and written by submissive man. Duties that differ from men granted souls, such as announcing this great story told. Each gospel writer shared so man will know, fulfilling prophecy told long ago. My words too echo those prophets penned down, Holy and Wonderful, I too had found. Worshipping high upon this earthly sky, behold this different than most human eye. I see a mother whom yet it occurred, embrace her son although He's holding her. Found highly favored, accepting her role, cradles the son who will cradle her soul. Providing nourishment from her young breast, feeding the body of man's living bread. I see a faithful new father protect, one with authority to resurrect. Soon he'll be teaching his carpenter's trade, to the creator of everything made. Yet my main focus remains on my Lord, once by His throne, now a baby adored. I stand a messenger sent by His name, yet now appear at this message which came. Joining my presence while singing loud praise, worship a baby these angels obey. Mankind's first Christmas seen from this stable, left His great throne seen by eyes of angels.

Finished with Writing

I'm finished with writing, my mind's overwhelmed. It told me this morning, rude words even yelled! I told my mind, "Listen, this is your fault! Thoughts come from you, every message you brought." Then came the nerve, my mind then blamed me, said, "Stop all the writing, please let me be." Our argument lasted an hour or two, more words got exchanged, the volume then grew. I finally turned, walked out of the room. My mind followed after; our fighting resumed. "Where are you going?" it said with such strife. Then I replied, "I too have a life. I will keep writing each thought you provide, keep yourself quiet and go back inside." Seeing its heartache, I paused for a while. Then said, spoke softly, "What's made you hostile?" "You're sharing my thoughts I privately hold. Writing them down without being told." I see mind's despair and hurt I had brought, not knowing before my mind was distraught. Apologies came once warring words broke, causing each one to quit, it's provoke. I realize now before I pen down, items held dear should not float around. I guess I was wrong to share every thought. This wonderful lesson my mind gladly taught. I'm finished with writing, so mind can go rest. I'm finished with writing, which my mind requests.

Hate to Read

I hate to read, therefore I write, 'cause what else could I do each night? A book's pages are too much read, that's why I write short poems instead. I have respect for all bookworms, but my brain wiring takes quick turns. Just what's so novel of tall tales, fake sailing seas while dodging whales? I'm fond of writings on true life, quick tales of joy, real hurt, and strife. Yet if I were to pen such text, just what could be my book's subject? Could my odd mind create fiction, or just speak my true conviction? If I so chose to share each fact, my pages would stand tall in stacks. There's one sure thing I know as true, I doubt I'd read the whole book through. It's possible I'd read it all, if pictures hid the words installed. Or maybe you could read to me, as long as you would let me sleep. I read all day while working long, so when I leave my brain is gone. I read each sign along the street, directive ones, some obsolete. I read instructions for each toy and read to both my little boys. I read the news upon my phone, which breaks my heart to read what's wrong. I read my mail but trash the ads, I read fun jokes that's made for dads. I read homework left on the floor, so why would I go read some more? I read sent text from family, the ones by friends but none from me. Maybe I should text myself, but that's more reading for myself. I guess I'll stick to writing these since I know how and hate to read.

Hateful

Dreadful is your presence while your actions are as rough. Friendship is desired by few because you make life tough. Unpleasantness that glares across this world with hostile eyes, reveal to us that deep within there's something you despise. Offensive words your tongue exhales with every breath you breathe and hands instead of helping move to author evil deeds. Your feet desire to walk a path that's dark as moonless night, refusing routes that's brightened by a useful source of light. You hide it well, this cause of pain; I wonder it's onset, a childhood voice that screamed abuse which you cannot forget? Or was the choice of agony brought forth void of motive, as you decide an awful life is one you'd rather live? A heart that you pretend is dark and loathe your own life's blood, yet secretly in private does desire to just be loved. If I could I'd take the hurt away and cast it far abroad, yet this large task is solely done by one whose name is God. I dare not lie that I have power to ease your misery, in honesty I claim although a friend you'll have in me. Remember this and understand that all men suffer pain, yet storing hurt's sour benefits will never keep one sane. I love you friend to tell you that your malice is fatal, a life of joy eliminates in you all that's hateful.

I Could

I could only dream that patience lives without a scream. I could only wish long waiting made my mind flourish. I could only hope my praying reached a higher slope. I could only dare strong self-control assist me care. I could only say when humbleness would come my way. I could only stand as pressure builds a violent hand. I could only thirst stark calmness quench me to love first. I could only want when others have to carry on. I could only yearn life suffering help my heart to learn. I could only urge myself the habits I must purge. I could only crave another soul distraught turn saved. I could only plead my efforts fill a struggling need. I could only long my conversation bring a song. I could only choose accepting moments I may lose. I could only need once seeking time upon each knee. I could only strive when serving One who is alive. I could only be if seeing more in life than me. I could only if I could only!

If I Were a Bird

If I were a bird, where would my wings fly? There isn't built highway far up in the sky! If I were a bird, which place could I soar? Through mountain valleys or cities explore? If I were a bird, I'd choose where to land. Places unknown in deserted islands. If I were a bird, what flock would be mine? Would I fly solo or stay in flock's line? If I were a bird, where would my nest lay? Built in a birdhouse or tree with decay? If I were a bird, I'd sing songs of praise as natural instruments melody plays. If I were a bird, when enemies came, I'd fly different patterns to harden their aim. If I were a bird, with clouds giving chance. I'd flutter all making silver lines dance. If I were a bird, in treacherous storms. I'd go on ahead with efforts to warn. If I were a bird, what could eyes obtain? Would they see beauty without mankind's pain? If I were a bird, who'd be a close friend? Would it be wildlife or only the wind? If I were a bird, I'd sit on fence posts, enjoying meadows which make calming hosts. If I were a bird, I'd fly my whole life. Soaking each morning the warming sunrise. If I were a bird, fed from divine hands, I'd not know God's grace of Salvation's plan. Although seeming free and precious in flight, I'd rather stand free in God's Holy sight.

Inadequate

One may define me not by this term, yet I through life most humbly did learn. Skills I attained throughout the long days, haven't found heights with many delays. Having errors in every task, "Where'd I go wrong?" is commonly asked. All work performed has fallen apart, some work I never wished I had start. Who is to blame, I'm guessing it's me. I'd argue myself, but I'd disagree. Why I can't do most anything right causes my mind to wonder each night. What I have touched will seemingly break, bringing out stress with awful heartache. How can I teach if I'm messing up, maybe go ask one more capable of. My mind works fine, yet slowly I learn, learning things quick is something I yearn. Found in the same of others I know, I'm not alone in learning things slow. My only fear is not that I fail, but that my family suffers as well. Men that provide and care just as I, hide the world's pressure each day they try. Though my desire is one passionate, I accept me as inadequate.

Jumping

Jumping hoops, jumping rope, jumping beans, and jumping smoke. Jumping feet, jumping brooms, jumping ship, and jumping wombs. Jumping high, jumping toys, jumping low, and jumping joys. Jumping jacks, jumping guns, jumping folks, and jumping fun. Jumping thoughts, jumping balls, jumping smooth, and jumping falls. Jumping up, jumping bugs, jumping down, and jumping hugs. Jumping frogs, jumping toads, jumping holes, and jumping roads. Jumping toes, jumping shoes, jumping fleas, and jumping views. Jumping pots, jumping pans, jumping on, and jumping spans. Jumping cows, jumping moons, jumping dance, and jumping spoons. Jumping rooms, jumping tunes, jumping spots, and jumping booms. Jumping fast, jumping slow, jumping seats, and jumping rows. Jumping fish, jumping worms, jumping snakes, and jumping germs. Jumping horse, jumping tails, jumping boards, and jumping whales. Jumping jumps, jumping humps, jumping dogs, and jumping rumps. Jumping cats, jumping mice, jumping rats, and jumping lice. Jumping blocks, jumping rocks, jumping clues, and jumping socks. Jumping brains, jumping games, jumping fools, and jumping flames. Jumping hearts, jumping farts, jumping slim, and jumping starts. Jumping, jumping all day long, jumping, jumping, I am gone.

Keep Your Head Down

Since I was a child and involved in events, I've suffered the loss at a game time's tough end. Instructions then came by intelligent men who experienced defeat time and again. "You gave it your best, but sometimes we all lose, remember this hurt and then strive to improve." Young ears so attentive, not one interrupts, they finished the talk with "Boys, keep your heads up." This same advice explained with tender great care from teachers when class was a struggle to bear. "Keep your head up, we all fail stressful tests, your mind's capable to conquer larger, hard quests." Soldier's exhaustion also merit the voice, "Keep your head up, son, there's no other life choice." Echoing loud sounds the drill sergeant's commands, "The battlefield needs not the weak but strong men." Encouragement came from both family and friends to stay positive when cruel people offend. As years have gone by, I've learned this powerful phase has been beneficial, one I'll continue to say. However, I've found a position more sure, that my head will hold when I have to endure. Prayer will do more than any words from the lips, of those who have faced the same troubling hardships. "Keep your head up," this world will strongly advise; "keep your head down" will be the words from the wise.

Labeled

You label me a "Christian," well, let me check my tag. That's exactly what it says, hey, would you look at that! I'm labeled as a "goody shoes," let me check those too. Goodness, would you look at that! It's written on them too. Labeled as a "bible thumper," I'll go look and see. I don't find a ding or dent; your thump was not by me. Labeled as a "holy roller," what's that even mean? I'll go look it up some time, then we'll reconvene. Labeled as a "hypocrite," this one really stings. Jesus Christ is not my name but still try living clean. Labeled as a "Jesus freak," now this one makes me laugh. What's your ideal precedence, one seeking cruel attacks? Labeled a "religious nut." Nah! Just misunderstood. Taste yourself then you will see the Lord is surely good! I just went and looked it up, your "holy roller" name. When was I seen in some "trance," that's not my worship's aim! Since I'm me and know me best, I'll label me for you. I am nothing but a man that love came to pursue. Just like you I make mistakes, yet thankful for His grace. That's my label and should show each day upon my face. I'm not better than no one and strive to show this true. I'm just saved and know I am and want the same for you. I don't label and will not but call me what you must. I will love you as does He, we're all just filthy dust. My desire is your label will read the same as mine. "Saved by grace," accepting His salvation plan's design.

Lay Hid

Painful abuse too often lay hid behind enclosed doors where escape is forbid. Below misery's roof silent voices lay hid contained by the cowardice fence's sharp grid. Lay hid among darkness is sufferings quiet cry, while questions arise in heart as to why. Lay hid in the presence of company's shield, fresh bruising that garments cloak secretly conceal. Upon the broad mirror is even lay hid, afflictions of heartache residing within. Written in ink lay hid on the page a new journals entry describing the rage. Appearing through windowpane lay hid a hopes dream that someone there walking would hear this loud scream. Lay hid in a casket then lowered six feet, a body now free from a life that was beat. Lay hid in the hearts outside the grave's gate, stand those who now realize their help is too late. Lay hid in the safety of Heaven's strong arm, a soul ever resting without no alarm. Lay hid on the bed behind a cell door are cowardly hands that won't hurt anyone.

Love's Face

"There is no beauty that we should desire," prophet's clean parchment with ink would acquire. Visage so marred, ol' Isaiah did pen, exceedingly worse than worn by living men. Beauty though found in a young virgin's eye, this mother whose heart once had pondered on why. An image first seen with eyes once held as blind, ever engraved in a man's heart and mind. Appearance of grace in lost souls He made whole, whose previous grip endured Satan's strong hold. Stained with His sweat and blood droplets he prayed, a kissed saddened face seeing righteous betrayed. His face fully bearded to fruitfully grow, plucked this cruel day by the hand of his foe. I read of His face, willing eyes did bestow! His crucifiers stand proudly below. A face never seen, a faith that I will, with longing eyes when death's breath I shall feel. Standing at death, waiting years may be more. Entering in through that Heaven's great door. Consider this thought of my last resting place, graciously bowed beside feet of Love's face.

Love's First Cry

Listeners lend ear, close listening eye, hear sounding sweet, loves falling cry. Stabled, cradled, swaddled with care, mother holds close, son she must share. Angel proclaimed, causing her fear, now sheds her first mother's love tear. Standing beside, living on faith, chosen favor, proud father's face. Herding pasture, shepherds tend flocks, peering amazed, as their livestock. Choir singing praise trumpet stars sky, angels cast broad, shepherds now cry. Glory to God, peace on the earth, good will to all, brought with this birth. Seeking with gifts, wise from the east, guided by light, worship this priest. Thirty-three years, spent without sin, now hung 'til death, my sin within. Below the cross, multitude stands, one mother cries, head in both hands. As she reflects, wondering why, recalls the time of her loves first cry. Buried to raise, risen to shine, shining abroad, seeking to find. Each sinful soul, knowing as I, recall with tears, His love's first cry.

Manger

Something seems different in my house tonight. Never an evening have stars shined such light. One through my stable door brightens my home, luminance path reveals I'm not alone. Silhouette shadows appear on my floor, shaped as the shepherds who've finished day's chore. Slowly each image become very clear, one suffers agony, one drying tears. Livestock who gaze toward this unique odd scene, question their purpose to lodge with unclean. Enters the moment each mother endures, birthing a child she now holding secures. Out in the distance angelic song heard, letting me know something greater occurred. Shepherds attending their flocks in the field, enter and worship this king now revealed. I'm just some worthless wood joined by few nails, why do I hold a king? What if I fail? How might a king use this wooden throne's hay, why not a golden throne, silver inlaid? Although unworthy, my bed humbly loan. Meant for a trough but today I'm a throne.

Old Kid

'Twas the night before Christmas when all through the house, not a creature was stirring except this old spouse. The stockings were hung by the chimney with care, in hopes that this Santa won't pull out his hair. The children were nestled all snug in the beds, as I hope instructions do not require meds. In the quiet darkness arose such a clatter, stumping my toe on a stinking toy tractor. Away to the sofa I flew like a flash, biting my finger 'til crying could pass. The moon on the breast of the new fallen snow, I gain composure and give it a go! When what to my wondering eyes should appear, a floor full of presents without more shed tears! I look to the chimney once more just in case Santa arrives for I'd slap his late face! Now Dasher, now Dancer, now Prancer and Vixen, on Comet—oh, crap, I forgot to fill stockings. A wink of my eye and a twist of my head, pinches my nerve as I climb into bed. I spoke not a word as I'm lying awake and think about memories the morning will make. Merry Christmas to all and to all a good night, ends this fun story which brought such delight. 'Twas the night before Christmas just like when first told. Exciting this old kid now forty years old!

One Day

God, I'm asking for one day, you remove this stabbing pain. I am asking for one chance, having joy to play and dance. Lord, I'm asking for my boys, they see Dad without hurt's noise. I ask also for my wife, so she'd see me enjoy life. God, if you could, while I work, have this pain no longer lurk. Just one day to rise from bed without aching in my head. To bend down and tie my shoe, void of pain I'd like to do. Lord, I wish to see the sky, yet when looking, I might cry. God, I wish to run just once, and it not feel like a punch. Just one day to clean my yard, without pain as a sharp barb. Lord, I'd love to fix my sink with no pain so I could think. I would love to turn my head without fear the turn I'd dread. God, what is this thorn of mine, teach me what you'd have me find. Lord, I trust your healing hand, though I don't quite understand. God, you know some hurt much more, help my mind to not ignore. Let myself be last in prayer, and these others have your care. Help my thoughts be unselfish, telling others your love's wish. Use this pain to let me shine, not complaining or to whine. I do know when asked you'll say, "I shall heal my child one day."

Or

Minutes turn quickly yet seconds slow down, hands counting sixty thus granting clock sound. Hours pass quicker while minutes prolong, creating gradually days swiftly gone. Days travel rapidly forcing long hours, procrastinating each year to expire. Years dissolve suddenly with lengthy days, bringing abruptly life's waiting new phase. Ears focus daily upon clocks tirade, listen as memories bitterly fade. Eyes view fresh calendars year after year, welcomes the future to soon disappear. Minds unaware what tomorrow shall bear, living as vapors that vanish in air. Years seeming shorter with days seeming long, days passing quickly with years dragging on. Each day perceiving as eternity, yet timeless day will each thousand years be. Patiently waiting for day to begin, returning soon as day quickly will end. Minute by minute, hour by hour, year after year will time seek to devour. Riddle me this, as such questions are asked, does time move slowly or does time move fast?

Saved From a Well

On fresh green meadows stand stories to tell, one most intriguing involves a deep well. Sit and reflect as this story begins, give your attention right down to its end. Once lived a donkey born stubborn with pride, plow hooked behind him yet work he denied. Placed out to pasture refusing commands, while other donkeys sweat workload demands. One day, while grazing, he sought to rebel, thought he'd escape yet jumped down a deep well. Now at the bottom knows this old rock wall, wasn't escape or his freedom at all. Thoughts quickly spin knowing his newfound fate, he should have listened yet knows that's too late. Pridefulness lead him to this darkened hole, asking for help but none come to console. Then he hears voices say this well is through. "We must now fill it then dig one brand new. His decayed body will cause us disease," heard by the donkey still screaming out pleas. As he stands shoulder deep in waters cool, something starts sprinkling his back seeming cruel. Sent by the shovel of each farmer's hand, evidence now surly death is soon planned. As the dirt mixes and forms a think mud, his fearful stomping is heard from above. He's working harder than ever before, and now discovers he's building a floor. Each mound of dirt that is meant for his death, he now is packing with determined breath. Slowly he sees that some progress is made, inching up higher no longer afraid. Those that are working now see with both eyes, from the deep darkness a hairy surprise. Close to the surface they frantically toss, slinging in branches, more dirt, even moss. Now midst his efforts exhaustion sets in, close to the top he pulls strength deep within. Finally working his way from the hole, falls to the ground as each farmer consoles. Here's now the lesson we learn from this act, when life's dumping dirt let's use it to pack! Then you'll be able to share and go tell, just as this donkey now saved from a well.

Silhouette

I am a silhouette, so what's the image I reflect? Is my outline shaped in love or formed with pride's neglect? I am a silhouette, so what's the object I portray? Am I filled with gentleness or brimming much decay? I am a silhouette, just what will gazing eyes perceive? Is my shadow kind to all or seeking to deceive? I am a silhouette, so what's the canvas I'm cast on? Do I lend a helping hand or each leave all alone? I am a silhouette, does darkness cover my whole page? Do I block the shining light or let the light on stage? I am a silhouette, so just what face do I reveal? Does a humbleness abide or selfish own ideas? I am a silhouette, so what is manifest in me? Does integrity show forth or honesty go flee? I am a silhouette, there is a face you need to see! Not the image of myself yet one who lives in me!

Ticktock

Tick…tock…tick…tock, now its twenty-seven minutes after night-time's two. In the darkened quiet soft sleep breaths repeat from you. Sharing with your rhythm clicks the ticking wooden clock. Leaving every second in the past with every tock.

Tick…tock…tick…tock, hand on fourteen minutes after this next hour of three. Calming heartbeat keeping time as your chest rests on me. Through the darkness time reveals as closely our hearts beat, Father Time will not allow this second to repeat.

Tick…tock…tick…tock, half past four now fills the air within still darkened room. Eyes begin to close in sleep, awake as ticks resume. Far away in dreamland you escape without one care, joining with the rhythmic beat is music from your hair.

Tick…tock…tick….tock, fifty-seven minutes gone with clock desiring dawn, body movements remind me I haven't been alone. As your body rises, it abstracts skin's added warmth, repositioned now alone as ticking still preforms.

Tick…tock…tick…tock, it's an hour later and the sunrise finds my face, ticking turns alarming as the dawn clock hands embrace. Sprayed aroma spreads its way across the morning's start, retrieves saddened memories it's time to soon depart.

Tick…tock…tick…tock, now the hour has arrived as life consumes the day. Ticking clock reverberates yet no ear hears it play. Sitting on the old nightstand continuing the time, ticks and tocks await until your body is near mine.

Tick…tick…tick…tock…

Washtub

Asleep in deep dream staring at a wood stove, crackles begin breaking into hot coals. Arriving with darkness comes moonlight's soft glow, coolness of air sneaking through old windows. Filthy young hands smelling as the worked pine, stacked in the corner tied with ragged twine. Melodious pinging the tin roof above, rain drops more soothing than of the home's love. Orange slices serve as provided quick meal; scent fills the room with each freshly pulled peel. Placed on the wood stove increasing the scent, reminds this young boy there's things still pleasant. Dreading the hour when this young boy will sleep, knowing harsh words wait which cause eyes to weep. This is no dream he then understands why, dreams should be pleasant and don't make you cry. Sink's running water is heard by his ear, carried then placed on the wood stove that's near. Slowly this water is warming to bathe, cleaning the pine gained from working all day. Once he is finished, he knows it will start, all of the painful words hurting his heart. Taking his time with each difficult scrub, hides by the safety brought by his washtub.

Why Can't I

Dorothy sang the measure why happy little bluebirds fly, high up in the rainbow sky questioning oh why can't I? I myself too question why, though desire is not to fly. My why stems from every wrong, burdened eyes see going on! Why can't I feed every child hungering or never smiled? Why can't I be wise to cure, patient's cancer they endure? Why can't I destroy each drug, so its user tastes true love? Why can't I build homeless homes, to avoid those throwing stones? Why can't I assist the hurt in each heart where pain does lurk? Life is not some lullaby yet resides this question why! Why can't I help broken homes, sharing help I too was shown? Why can't I see others care, seeming blind to earth's despair? Why can't we see past our needs, petty things as others bleed? Why can't I remove the cry, of those asking themselves why? Why can't I just close my eyes, fall asleep, not asking why? Why, oh, why, oh, why, oh, why, why has love went so awry! Why can't I diminish hate, why are many so irate? Why can't I, time's drawing nigh, make a difference in a life! There's a land built way up high that red slippers can't supply. Some will enter, more will try, turn and question why can't I?

Wish I Could Be Part of That World

I understand not how a mermaid had joy to dwell in a land that man would destroy. I ask myself what did she see in people 'cause I look around and just see their evil. The sea is most violent at times, I am sure, but cannot compare to the pain some endure. Sure, we have gadgets and gizmos to use, but some exploit them in committing abuse. Plenty of thingamabobs made for us all, snarfblatts and dinglehoppers, short and some tall. Items most useful for us in this life, yet even these items in greed stir up strife. Some even having the unconcerned nerve, toss trash to the ground on a highway's blind curve. That's how she ended up having these goods since keeping creation clean is misunderstood. Deceit in the sea she even got trapped yet found on the shore lives a much worse attack. I guess in our hearts we each have a desire escaping to lands we'd much rather acquire. For me though, I know by accepting God's son a place is awaiting when this race I've run. What bothers me most is there's also a place intended for demons yet some soon will face. Sounding out loud when their soul is then hurled, wish I could be part of that world.

Writer's Block

I am having writer's block, what wise words could I write? How can I go write at night when all my words go hide? Come here, little wordy words, it's time for us to play! I am seeking words today, there's thoughts we need to say! Did you grow a pair of feet then quietly step away? Or go board a boring plane and fly somewhere to stay? I sure hope you didn't plunge far in a deep dark hole, while out jogging with new feet or taking a long stroll. We love songs so did you place yourself within a verse? If that's so, then sing your song but next time ask me first! Did you book a trip with books to hang out with book friends? I can understand your wish but each book has an end. Please don't tell me you're involved with words in the wrong crowd! We agreed that's not allowed, this promise we have vowed. Has there been a word napping, and is the ransom small? Who would dare to steal my words, I freely share them all! Did you find a better home where words are greater said? Surely, you've been happy with the home that's in my head! What if my cruel writers block blocked my words in block walls? Maybe I could break them out if blocks were not built tall! It could be that with new feet they stepped into concrete. Lingered there without a care now forming a feet street. Could it be they don't like me or how I used them all? Surely that thought isn't true, from what my thoughts recall. What if fame became their name while leaving me the same? Could I claim and so proclaim, my words must not be changed? Maybe soon their attitude will find my brain and knock, ending all the agony caused from this writer's block.

As a Child

Just today, I traveled to the playground of my youth, evidence exposing such a blatant saddened truth. In my mind resides the lie, it's just as I recall. Yet I know what time has shown, it wasn't that at all. As my eyes close seeing the fond playground I once knew, there the winding metal slide and swing set quickly grew. Children laughing join the scene as I turn to survey, there I find my former friends who freely run and play. I then see me half the size just like my mind retained, living with a childhood love this playground had ingrained. Through the woods I view a group now playing kick the can, someone launched it far away now all the prisoners ran! Such a smile this playground dream created in my life, being my escape from all the worldly pain and strife. Now my opened eyes stand seeing this large playground shrink, how could this transition come by way of one eye's blink. As I leave while reminiscing of each hour played, lives the truthful wishing thought reality forbade. If I could fill one last day with memories compiled, I'd walk through this playground gate returning as a child.

Asleep on This Lion

Darkness abundantly crowding this den, daylight unable these stone walls ascend. Coldest of shivering brought by chilled stone, scattered debris echoes sounds of dead bone. Hands become eyes navigating void light, claws scrape the stone floors now killing the quiet. Raised hair protruding each neck follicle, as warm foul breathing blows invisible. Ears hear another breath in my foreground, then pants a third while breaths circle around. Arms reaching forth seek position to sleep, finding a bed with rough fur made unique. Nearing exhaustion with eyelids heavy, rings unexpectedly words heavenly. "Praying with faith your voice thrice sought the Lord, rest till the morning where you'll leave restored." Eyes close with soothing breaths from this pillow, raising just slightly then falling down low. Sounds from the entrance awaken each eye, morning sun shining as each realize. Seeing the eyes of each schemer widen, finding me safe while asleep on this lion.

Chicken Wing

Say I interpret a chicken's sweet dream, disguised a chicken to know chicken things. What would they think and could chickens conspire, keeping each chicken from reaching a fryer? Is this loud clucking their chicken speech code, signal discreetly for crossing the road? Such a great mystery, why they cross roads, maybe one chicken can share what it knows. Maybe they all desire being supreme, although I find that thought slightly extreme. One thing for certain that I need to check is the odd movement each does with its neck. The mother chicken's love must be splendor, one diddle's mom was known being tender. Then I encountered a chicken not nice, it must have hatched with its own chicken spice. Slowly I learn of the chicken lifestyle, some being spoiled though most chickens seem mild. I found the secret of each chicken's dream, as I completed my chicken spy scheme. Each chicken wishes just as I too dream, all chickens seeking to be chicken wings! They also know what I've known for so long, chicken wings always requiring a bone. No, ma'am, I don't want the boneless bucket, those are not wings that's a dang chicken nugget!

First Breath

Breath by a mother transferred to her womb, feeding a precious life arriving soon. Breath becomes heavy as labor ensues; childbirth then finished thus breathing renews. Heard through exhaustion and filling heart depths, cries ringing loud of her infant's first breath! Quickly her newborn blooms into her child, holding each breath when falls become complied. Now her exhaustion comes not from a birth, yet from sweet motherhood proudly observed. Breaths in her morning and breaths through her day, breaths in the evening with breaths left to pray. Her child now older soon leaving this home, breaths hiding heartache which also has grown. Her empty house provides silence to hear, each sobbing lonely breath brought with shed tear. Years begin passing while memories surmount, each breath expelled are too many to count. Difference appears with her feeble new age; breaths emerge heavy with each turning page. Just as her baby once needed love's care, now time approaches she'll need her child there. Body turned weak she so earnestly gasps, roles now reversed with her baby's hand grasp. Whispering, "Lord, You prepared me for death, bring this child's mother to breathe her first breath!"

First Church Day

I never sang written psalms in a choir, singing the song of sin was my desire. I never worshipped in a synagogue, enjoying times rather away from God. I never sought the built Temple to pray, offering no lamb every atonement day. Scripture, I heard by each prophet of old, claiming Messiah for Israel foretold. Until this day, I rejected such claim, now on death's mountain three malefactors hang. First, I joined mocking then I saw his eyes, unlike this thief who had eyes of disguise. I could perceive he looked further within, seeing the guilt of my unconfessed sin. Now blinded eyes came to understand why, three wooden crosses held men soon to die. Two were found guilty convicted by law, one choosing death giving freedom to all. Asking with final breaths when my time comes, remember me entering your great kingdom. He gave the promise of sweet paradise, my first church day came right after I died!

Future Eyes

Blue eyes sit viewing a dull fading sight, framing this portrait of old black and white. Sweet moment captured now frozen in time, dated by quill's ink in nineteen o' nine. On the frame back is the same name just as, he which is holding this old photo has. A foreign face unfamiliar to him, has striking features with body's frame slim. Through his young mind rolls the questioning thought of this occasion the camera had caught. With this inquisitive unknown he seeks, comes the remembrance of pictures he keeps. Those of his children and some from his youth, few showing falsehoods with most having truth. Some scenes forgotten but mainly he knows each moment captured that his photo shows. Many pose family enjoyments in life, recalling days he could greatly describe. His photo book also pictures a love of individuals death took above. Lastly, he understands what he can't see, "What future eyes will be looking at me?"

Harp upon the Willow

Melodies conduct my day; emotions play their song. Notes of praise with joyful sways, each measure lifting wrongs. Instrumental healing soothes world's painful wounds deep gash, also self-inflicting shames that wear sackcloth and ash. Heart's desire for harmony is singing each refrain, repetitious rhythmic peace this mind hopes to maintain. Not just I, yet let this choir continue vocally, as our great conductor stands and leads so faithfully. Orchestrated sections of mankind aspire their note, whether strings or woodwinds as percussion beats are smote. Music upon mountains echo loudly at twin's peak, yet deep darkened valleys is where songs should not grow weak. Even caught in wilderness where evil mocks my song, enemies determine they want all this music gone. Keeping faith to journey home desiring stanza's flow, never hanging my song's harp upon the old willow.

I Am Normal

I am normal, I suppose. I have asked, yet no mind knows. I assume you each eat soup, adding peanut butter too! I suspect that when you wipe, you pull four squares just as I. Unless it was single ply, folding six for safe apply. (Wink!) I guess each one counts the time, brushing teeth as I do mine. I'm sure you eat on the dot, eight and twelve then six o'clock. With both off, I bet you too, tuck your laces in each shoe. When I read, I read out loud, helping my brain stick around. I presume you read the same, since we're normal, unashamed! I admit I don't chew ice, just like you I loathe that vice. I imagine you're a fan, loving bluegrass as this man! Hold up now, what's this I hear? Surely, you have spoken unclear! You don't have these charming quirks? I thought all lived not diverse! I guess that makes me not you, making you not me…who knew? Now I see what normal means. We're each human, not machines!

I Don't Know

I don't know you anymore, once my mom I now ignore!
I don't know you as my dad, who stood proud now rather sad.
I don't know my brother now, asking me relentless how?
I don't know my sister too, who I'm telling I hate you.
I don't know my children's life, as I share my little lies.
I don't know my spouse at all, losing trust when I don't call.
I don't know my childhood friend, since I chose our bond should end.
I don't know my family, who I'd rather not go see.
I don't know my life choices, hide my ears from their voices.
I don't know myself or mind, leaving each hug far behind.
I don't know when I hear truth, hating words which I should do.
I don't know a home resides, turning from each love inside.
I don't know these drugs cause pain to my body and my brain.
I don't know how I don't know. Please help me know I don't know.

I Hail From...

I hail from Switzerland, Bär is my name! Forced out when cruel persecution had come. Zürich our country where farming was life, before the state church cast troublesome strife. Raised Anabaptist refusing false ways, standing while fighting for truth of the faith. Hans Jakob Bär was determined to sail, desiring worship without facing jail. Crossing the ocean fulfilling his goal, found Pennsylvania which settled his soul. Living in freedom to worship his Lord, finding a country he greatly adored. Then a descendent somehow found the way, down to Ashe County to settle and pray. As I get older, I respect these men, without their strength just where would have I been? Hoping to visit in Zürich someday, seeing a land chosen never to stay. Maybe I'll find some remaining kinfolk, visit the grave of those fallen provoked. I am so thankful my title is Bare. Know who you are and how you settled there.

I Hate This Cow

A prodigal not, as I remain home. Ignore that brother which selfishly roams. I abide faithful while working this land, performing duties my father commands. I possess wisdom unlike his young son. See my accomplishments, each that I've done. My estate portion contains every jewel, contrary to that young riotous fool. I observe father now resting from chores, gaze the horizon, my efforts ignored. I toil and labor with each law obeyed, yet he keeps seeking the son gone astray. I even follow the order to feed this single calf although seeing no need. What in his heart should envision return, by my spoiled sibling not proving concern? He should accept just as I but instead, he has determined his son isn't dead. He also safely keeps guarded to gift, the finest robe incase prodigal lives. Not only cloth but new shoes for his feet, ring fabricated and this calf to eat. Daily I pass by this barn door and turn, saying my brother will never return. Then I continue while questioning how, he grants forgiveness as I hate this cow!

I Was the Stone

I was the stone where laws were penned, authored words man would offend. Prior to death one must atone, versed as written on this stone.

I was the stone which David held, this Goliath I impaled. Prior to death I was unknown, versed now as a killing stone.

I was the stone robed hypocrites, meant to stone adultery with. Prior to death by grace alone, versed her sin's forgiving stone.

I was the stone that sealed death's tomb; outside me, great sorrow loomed. Prior to death, love left His throne, versed eternal victory's stone.

I was the stone by Stephen's brow, thrown by persecution's house. Prior to death, I laid not thrown, versed now as a martyr's stone.

I was the stone which filled your heart, cast by Satan's evil dart. Prior to death sin went condoned, versed saved by the Cornerstone.

Language

I accept most English words, except confusing terms. Like this morning around eight, I ate with great concerns! Finishing my cereal with only milk to drink, every thought seemed serial, too many thoughts to think. If you're thinking I'm insane I guess your point of view, is to know in saying no when such thoughts visit you. Maybe my mind isn't fair assuming others don't think the same while paying fare in sailing right along. Maybe they write just as I, with selling what they pen, or hang up great literature on walls with small push pins. If you only knew those thoughts I had new every day, you would learn a lesson that may lessen minds delay. Speaking of all words which would and should compile your brain, you could stack them high like piles of wood kept from the rain. Then the idle thoughts could reign supreme as idols vain, sowing out confusing thoughts as wisdom sewing veins. Fields now filled with sensors keeping me from writing wrong, I applaud those censors keeping wise discernment strong. I still doubt most every word released within my mind yet won't steal an author's words from other written lines. Patience is required to think as many essays roll, like a patient's waiting role for results to be told. My desire is those who read my stories plainly heed, every single thought while holding tightly like a reed. If I took a poll of those consistent reading me, just where on their totem pole would my poem writings be? What I write may seem off course yet walk past every peak. That coarse path will smoothly pass then minds can take a peek. All these English words arrive with many, piece by piece, then create a language I request translate to peace!

Men Don't Read Poems

Men don't read poems. We're too tough, as we fight and spit or fuss!
Who needs writings or a brain, when there's cars and trucks or trains?
We like playing in the dirt, fishing, hunting, all experts. We like flirting with our girl, let them write for all the world. Men like working with some grease, as with food, yes add grease please! Intellect is no concern; thinking is not very fun. Give us sports with a few snacks, while we bend and show our cracks. No we care not to go read yet go watch a boxer bleed. Our heads are meant just for hats, or a friendly punching tap. Why would we read some poem wrote, when we're holding our remote? Let the sissies rhyme some words, while we talk of our large turds. Then we'll fart and fall asleep, without thinking very deep. We just mention to the dog of our worries and what's wrong. Next, we'll keep those troubles hid, then go play just as big kids. Building stuff is what we do, give us nails and wood with glue. Pens and pencils only job is for cleaning earwax clogs. We don't read since we're too cool, just like when we sat in school. Let's go race then shoot some guns. Men don't read poems, that's so dumb.

My Brain

My brain sees a different scene than most minds that behold, visualizing stories from a viewpoint rarely told. Such the image of our Lord shown hanging on His cross, my eyes view quite vividly a cross which sadly talks. Or sharp brightness from the time in darkness giving light, I observe the minutes lost and what this clock would write. I too see society not understand true love, so I write of prideful eyes that's spilling hateful blood. I too hear a separate sound which someone may not know, like an alcoholic drown when hearing rivers flow. Also from the soft breathing of children fast asleep, echoes sound of peaceful dreams and memories they will keep. I have heard a falling shoe then pictured the last step, of my Savior's sandals tossed aside which loudly wept. My odd mind will also smell a growing Fraser fir, then I find myself beside a washtub to immerse. Smelling the deep salty sea as my friend fights cancer, in the darkened stormy edge is where my mind transfers. Every sense contributing an interesting thought, as my brain securely keeps them locked within its vault. Then my fingers use the key while bringing to the page, my desire in writing poems that maybe create change.

My Sister's Mother's Son

Life provides the brother's song that many brothers sung, not one verse but singing two, which voices both old and young. Introduction music playing my first sister's verse, duet now created with sweet harmony immersed. Lyrics of her caring soul ring firm soft melody, as her mind with rhythm strong holds songs of memory. Known to show emotions held while voicing every thought, held her brother close nearby and always for him fought! Now the instrumental brings my second verse to sing, as my little sister turns our duet song to three. Lyrics of her innocence create a lullaby, ringing loud the high measure of notes in great supply. Just as stubborn as the two which sing this brother's song, our trio will always bring acoustics loud and strong! Written in the sibling chorus of this endearing hymn, lives a love unbreakable and joy filled within them. Closing out the final note this brother sang before, he again desires request for singing an encore. Once my curtain closes and the orchestra is done, I'll cherish the title as my sister's mother's son.

Naps

Jesus napped so I will too, on my couch in socks and shoes! Sometimes I nap in my bed, with my dog beside my leg. I have even napped outside, in the shade and in sunshine. Working hard permits some rest, mostly while I'm at my desk. Finding sleep when raising kids, seems as if sleep went and hid. Yet my naps while holding each, are the best naps I have reached. I wish I could drive my truck, fall asleep then wish for luck. Even naps out on the beach are superb when nap's complete. I could even nap at church, but I enjoy to worship. I would love just one full day, on my pillow in the hay. You may never want a nap, aren't you just a restful chap! What would be a charming treat, is if I could nap and eat. Once I napped out in the woods, all alone and napping good. I once never took a nap, looking back man what the crap! Now I nap each time I can, could I now be an old man? Even when I'm watching sports, goodness I'm way out of sorts. I would go nap with my wife, yet we have a busy life. I will lay beside her soon, but we still won't have much room. We have kids which like our bed, more than us it seems instead. This could be why I need sleep, and to why my eyes are weak. Life has come as I adapt to my life of needing naps!

Older than Dad

Our first-born baby, now aged twelve years old, won as a puppy by raffle that sold. You aren't much larger than when you were born, yet you make loving the largest love worn. Chewing my door jams the first week at home, rather than chewing your own little bone. Then your desire grew to stealing my socks, chasing you down the small hallway a lot. It was a joy training you to potty, walking outside just my baby and me. Somehow our bed then became also yours, leaving the purchased one still on the floor. Wanting to play one more time before bed, you start your growling while shaking your head. Then after fighting and needing some rest, you laid beside me and took a deep breath. Slowly you pawed with the sweetest intent, wanting a rub until you felt content. Rides on the parkway, your eyes so alert, face in the vent as a cooling dessert. Joining along with each vacation trip, seeing the beaches and mountainous tips. Then came the birth of our precious born sons, although quite nervous you welcomed each one. Growing accustomed to having them here, became a mommy and made it quite clear. Setting your boundaries with love and such care, showed them affection that we knew was there. Now more excitement exists in our home, looking at how our blessed family has grown. Yet in my heart I see something that hurts, you're losing much of the youthfulness quirks. No longer able to jump into bed, waiting for someone to lift you instead. I've even seen the hard struggle you have, just to come sit on the couch in my lap. Seeing small moments of you acting young, still makes me smile knowing you're having fun. Though in my mind there's the knowledge quite sad, my little baby's now older than dad.

One Eye Sees

My eyes need no crystal ball nor wicked tarot cards, for one sees what's beautiful as one sees hurtful scars. One eye sees man's act of greed in gaining futile wealth, while small children lay there starving, die in fecal filth. One eye sees quite opposite in those who sacrifice, hearts which barely have enough still give to save a life. One eye sees addiction's hold destroy a bright future, causing mind's deceptive lies to never seek a cure. Yet the other sees a life pulled from the needle's track, stretching forth supporting arms to users still attacked. One eye sees ungodly hate instilled within man's heart, without caring evilness has torn mankind apart. One eye cries in seeing such despicable cruel ways, but one sees pure Godliness in heart's loving arrays. One eye sees a selfish lust committing immoral acts, making trust an issue where relationships can't last. Yet I see a man and wife embrace on their deathbed, faithful to each other sixty years since both hearts wed. Asked by one the other day, "You sure a God exists?" My reply was "Can't your eyes see love among conflicts? Open both to understand this truth of love and hate, man's intentions naturally aren't eyes that love creates."

Peaceful Eyes

Now I lay me down to sleep, child secure in dream's mystique. Father's mind desires to know, where his precious child's dream goes. Speculation soon arrives, will his impact there survive? Does this dream include the man, still embracing his child's hand? Can this young child's sleeping eye, view a father's love inside? Is it likely this dreamland, drowns this man with sinking sand? Heartache fills his troubled soul, praying this thought isn't so! Coming forth from his own eye, this child's father's tears reply. "I view peace in your closed eyes," deep sleep breathing sighs imply. Living safe within your dream, resting in a loving scene. Finding there your father's care, knowing love he'll always share. Ears attend his words aloud, voiced again, "My child, I'm proud." Echoed further in dreamland, reassurance seen firsthand. Evidence this loving child, knows a father's loving smile. Ending soon night's dreamy sleep, daylight's love again repeats. Now this father finds his bed, with closed eyes, he bows his head. Tiring father does the same, as the child who shares his name. Reaching out his father's hand, grasping one who understands. God his Father wants to see, peaceful eyes as children sleep.

Shed Skin

Ssslowly I ssslither acrosss sssoftened sssoil, ssseeking sssince sssun-light prey sssubstance to coil. Sssoundless sssure progresss through grassesss unssseen, ssseing ssso sssavory sssweet sssuitable ssscenes. Sssafely sssecuring by sssinking sssharp fangsss, sssliding sssnared sssupper now sssuffocating. Sssalty sssensational ssswalloed sucesss, sssatisfied ssssteady to sssunbathe and ressst. Sssecretly sssheding sss-kin sssimply to ssshape, ssscaling myssself to a sssly bigger sssnake.

The Crow

Interesting creatures teach us lessons of value. We must pay attention, forming attributes each choose. Case in point, the friendly crow dressed in majestic black, symbolizing transformation by their wiser acts. First observe compassion they exhibit to their own, mournfully attending funerals of crows passed on. Next is great abilities to fashion useful tools, with knowledge unlike some who've studied much in schools. How's this talent possible inquisitive minds ask? With the largest ratio of brain to body mass! Crows will even drop a nut before a passing car. Which will break the outer shell then leave food to devour. Crows can learn our language if investing time is made, having conversations with mankind now unafraid. Yet the trait I most admire about this special bird, is the kindness they express which mankind needs to learn. Showing thankfulness to those who kindly provide food, crows deliver presents to that giver now confused. Maybe, oh, just maybe, what each need for love to grow, comes the question is our acts exampled like the crow?

The Garden of My Mind

Fenced within mind's tendencies variety is sown, seeds containing holy thoughts and wicked motives thrown. Daily battles planted by the fleshy hand of wrong, while the other cultivates where righteous sows thereon. Planted seeds of jealousy regretfully get dropped, yet some optimistic seeds which hope men land atop! Greedy seeds too reach the ground where selfish wants may grow, as strong seeds of charity root further down below. Prideful seeds have left this hand pretentiously in vain, as seeds having humbleness assist not to complain. Bitter seeds so secretly sprout blinding hostile eyes, where forgiving seeds belong so hearts won't grow despise! Cluttered in this basket mind resides a worried seed, mixed among the promises of comfort guaranteed! Incoherent lustfulness propelled into the soil, yet pure seeds of faithfulness grow lasting care unspoiled. Hateful seeds stir up terrain while spilling painful acts, while true loving seeds produce substantial life impacts. Slothful seeds consuming idle hands caught in a snare, while the active seeds remind all moments demand prayer. Daily harvest time ensures both choices I shall find, yet which fruit is gathered from the garden of my mind?

The United States on Nothing

We, the people of the United States on Nothing, in order to form a more divided Union, ignore Justice, insure domestic hostility, divorce our own common defense, demote the general Welfare, and destroy the Blessing of Liberty to ourselves and end Prosperity, do evade this Constitution of the United States of Whoever We Are. All Legislative Powers herein granted shall be wicked in a Congress while dividing States, which shall demise a Senate and Haughty Representatives. The House of Representatives shall be transposed to morons chosen every second by deception to several States, and the Electors in each State shall have no qualifications. The Senate of the Divided States shall be imposters from each State, chosen with no legislative concern, for decades and each Senator shall have no brain. Immediately after they shall be determined in Collusion with questionable Elections, they shall be divided eternally and maintain no class. All debts compromised and derangements entered into, before the Adoption of this Constitution, shall be always against the United States under its Constitution, enjoying Confrontations.

From a Concerned Citizen.

Torn Apart

Oh, Jerusalem! I have hung some thousand years now draped upon your hill, first your tabernacle now this temple viewing guilt. My eye west this curtain veil beheld your natural sin, yet my eye upon the east found mercy's love within. You see spilling blood discharge from sacrificing meat, while I witness your high priest approach the mercy seat! My fine cloth embroidered skirt with cherubim's large wing, separates this Holy place from what is deemed unclean. Chaos now erupting in the temple judgement hall, yet this lone offender stands without reply at all. Something of His presence seems familiar to my cloth, could this be the Holy one fulfilling given law? Great commotion leaves the room as verdict is proclaimed, knowing of prophetic truth my duty soon will change! Evidence my labor's end is closely drawing near, sounded by the ripping flesh from whips outside I hear. Then again, the promise that the sacrifice arrived, comes from chanting in the crowd so loudly crucify! Now suspended just as I yet hanging from a cross, on a different hill as midday sunlight rays are lost. "I commend my spirit," sounds the final words declared, as the earth starts quaking while I feel my fabric tear. Understanding what took place I saw this final lamb, offer His own body though He was the great I Am! I'm no longer useful as full access now can start, to this Holy Father by two bodies torn apart!

Unconcern Seen

Unconcern seen by eyes deep asleep, mankind as ants clog each busy street. Normalcy hides truth loudly proclaimed, yet I peer now at souls which remain. Unknown that just one eye blink before, sounds rang aloud with trumpet ignored. I then observe a mother distraught, search for her child this rapture has caught. Screams of distress grow loud from her mouth, "If you're hiding, quit playing! Come out!" Then my eyes view a husband in bed, clinching a book his wife always read. As her night clothes lay where she just slept, he lays in flooding tears where he's wept. At this same hour a wailing consumes, doctors who serve a nursery room. Once filled with each new baby just birthed, now beside me above the sad earth. Scattered across the land and deep sea, planes and long trains burn crashing debris. At a ship's stern, its captain once stood. Leaving the crew who wished he still could. In a rest home where two shared a suite, lives only one alone in her seat. Staring with fear, remembering the talks, at her roommate's old hung pictured cross. Texting a friend without a response, I see a teen whose phone quickly drops. Chaos ensues, destruction begins! Broadcasting news claim this ain't the end. At his pulpit, a preacher of lies, stands to address as followers cry. Floating back down to my empty bed, cry for the souls so sadly misled. As I awake from this awful dream, I still observe that unconcern seen.

Visitation Hour

Counting sheep while wide awake and numbering each leap, as your memory also jumps inside my eyes which weep. Only pictures show your face upon these moonlit walls, as the brightness radiates your smile I still recall. Within darkened silence sounds faint laughter in my mind, echoing a melody that only love designed. Moonlight now revealing wrinkled hands I cannot hold, as the jumping sheep become a never-ending fold. Nighttime minutes slowly tick as moonlight fades away, as remembering every word I never got to say. Wishing eyes would close in sleep so I could speak with you, and explain the heartache brought when your sweet life was through. Needing your great wisdom while I struggle to maintain, without you beside me life will never be the same. Though it is impossible if I obtained such power, I'd request that Heaven grant a visitation hour!

Where Is My Daddy

I am starting school today, beginning with pre-K! Daddy couldn't make it; he is busy. It's okay. What a great first year and goodness how it went so fast, I'll be heading back real soon to kindergarten class. My new teacher asked today to draw my family. Asking me, "Who is this man?" I said, "That's my daddy!" In the morning, I begin my first day of first grade, Daddy said he'd come some time and see things that I made. Now I'm starting second grade and know this coming year, I will see my daddy come and visit with me here. Third grade is much harder, but I won the science fair. I looked for my daddy but just saw his empty chair. I hate fourth grade really bad and got into a fight, Momma had to pick me up since Dad's too drunk to drive. How come other daddies come to every school event? I am in the fifth grade, but I haven't seen him yet? Middle school is terrible, but I found friends like me, we meet in the bathroom drinking liquor like Daddy. I'm expelled from high school, and I'm never going back. Now I get to see my dad when we go buy some crack. This is my first night in jail, it's worse than any school. Yet I wonder if my daddy thinks his son is cool. Asking my attorney as we enter the courtroom, "Do you think my daddy will be showing up real soon?" I was sentenced to prison for twenty years today, but you know one stupid thing you'll never hear me say? As I sit and study to obtain my GED, I don't even care to ask, "Hey, where is my daddy?"

Where's the Rain

Cloudless sky around earth's sin, day and night since sin begin. Moisture given by ground's dew, this provision nearly through. One stands righteous among men, unjust others breaking trend. "Where's the rain, you insane fool?" starts year one of ridicule. Wickedness and violence swell, hearts of men extend rebel. Noah stands proclaiming truth, once again the people choose. Year now ten, misunderstood, forms and shapes strong gopher wood. "Flesh corrupt shall not prevail, once this vessel sets a sail!" Heard replies cause saddened pain, "You're erratic, where's the rain?" Marching kinds come two by two; opposition continues. Many years have now elapsed, since the warning loud was cast. "Where's the rain?" with mocking laughs, final goods are getting stacked. Walking through the open door, sounds the invite just once more! Yet each turn and walk away, choosing sinful death's decay. From inside all ears obtain, the last mock of "Where's the rain?" Clear skies sudden grow as dark, pounding hands attack closed Ark. Cries now heard among the sound, lightning, thunder, bursting ground. Bodies drown in waters deep; souls discover torment's weep. Roaring out consumed by flame, screams for mercy, "Where's the rain?"

Why Stars Shine Each Night

Minds reason different why stars shine each night, thoughts yet acknowledge this beautiful sight! Sailors encompass sky's consistent grid, mapping clear bearings avoiding storms hid. Eyes from astrology seeking a sign, survey positions as why stars align. Minds of astronomy analyze spheres, measurements only accounting light years. Even the astrophile caught in desire, stands upon hours delighted to stare. Though having knowledge much larger than mine, science can't contain every aspect divine. Certainty found in clear unblinded eyes, holding a wisdom to understand why. Seen by these eyes hangs a perfect made sky, each orbit stationed maintaining all life. No cosmic blast could just happen to place, heavenly bodies set perfect in space. Wise view the darkened night sky's starry sea, knowing within dwells One greater than me. Excellent beauty of light coming forth, expelling darkness so life stays on course. Lying awake through tough troublesome times, finding a comfort in starry designs. I do not question why stars shine each night, knowing the purpose to bring hearts delight!

About the Author

Scotty Bare is a North Carolina native, raised in the beautiful north-western mountain county of Ashe. Growing up in this small-town environment, he was taught the value of faith in God along with a great importance of love and dedication to family. Although facing times of adversity, as so many in this mountain community, he learned the enduring significance of laughter. Each experience developed within his mind the creative ability in expressing true emotions about his spiritual, physical, and mental life through poetry, to which he determined to share with hopes to enlighten and encourage individuals in their own life's endeavors.

He currently resides in the foothills of North Carolina, where he met his lovely wife, Rosanna, who provides positive encouragement for his desire to write. Scotty is a father to two vivacious, kind-hearted young sons, who contribute numerous writing material almost on a daily basis! He currently serves as a deacon and choir director of Pleasant Grove Baptist Church where he enjoys worshipping his Heavenly Father alongside his family while rejoicing in the salvation through Christ that he received at the age of ten. His desire in writing is that each reader's mind would be inspired when contemplating each joy and struggle life produces.

9 798891 129986